Dr. and Mrs. Nasser Lotfi with daughter Elizabeth in Cologne, Germany.

IRANIAN CHRISTIAN

NASSER LOTFI

WORD BOOKS
PUBLISHER
4800 WEST WACO DRIVE
WACO, TEXAS
76703

This book is dedicated to my
Moslem mother,
MOHTARAM,
who has always given me unconditional
love, even though she could not
understand my decision to become
a Christian.

Iranian Christian
Copyright © 1980 by Word, Incorporated, Waco, Texas.

Unless otherwise indicated, Scripture quotations are from the
New American Standard Bible, copyright 1960, 1962, 1963, 1968,
1971 by the Lockman Foundation, used by permission.

ISBN 0-8499-0275-4
Library of Congress Catalog Card Number 80-52310

Printed in the United States of America.

Contents

Acknowledgments

My sincere gratitude goes to those many Christian brothers and sisters who encouraged and prayed for me during the writing of this book.

I wish to express my deep gratitude to my Christian brother, Dr. Tony Ash of the Institute for Christian Studies, Austin, Texas, for his generous assistance in the final editing of the manuscript and for his numerous helpful suggestions.

I especially thank Brother Jack Taylor and Brother Manley Beasley for their spiritual guidance and prayers far away in Interlaken, Switzerland, and then back again in Texas.

Special gratitude goes also to a dear person who helped me immeasurably but who preferred not to be named here.

Next, I extend warm thanks to Mrs. Carolyn Huffman and Mrs. Peggy Dunlap for their encouragement and Christian concern.

I deeply thank my dear wife, Marion, who shared her knowledge with me so that this book grew even richer. She was my first editor, my typist, my prayer companion, and my daily encourager.

Last and most of all, I thank my Lord God for his hand and guidance in this work. I praise him for all these people whom he sent my way to help me. To God be all the glory!

N.L.

Foreword

With roots imbedded deeply within the traditions of Islam, Nasser Lotfi came to faith in Jesus Christ as the promised Messiah. Here is a volume which traces those roots and allows the reader to follow along on the exciting journey.

Provided here is a keen insight into Islam traditions and customs foreign to ours in the Western world. This insight is desperately needed in a world of misunderstanding and hate.

With the proliferation of pressures in the Middle East and the revival of fanatical missionary zeal among the Moslem world it is of utmost importance that the Moslem mentality be understood. The message of Islam is now believed by upwards of three-quarters of a billion people with missionary plans on virtually every continent. It is vital that we learn how to present Christ to the Moslem mind with a heart of love. We can no longer disregard this segment of the world. It has come to us. Nasser's report that there are more than two million Moslems in the United States is shocking.

Here is the superbly told story of one Moslem's journey to Jesus and his commitment to the reaching of his countrymen with the gospel.

The chapter containing a theoretical dialogue between a Moslem and a Christian is a classic and should be carefully examined by any person desiring to effectively witness to the child of Islam.

I am glad that Nasser Lotfi has done this work and I predict for it a wide and effective outreach.

Jack R. Taylor
President, Dimensions in Christian Living

Preface

Nasser Lotfi has a fascinating story to tell, and in this book he tells it in a most engaging way. It is worth reading simply for the sake of the events themselves. It is made the more fascinating because it is a pilgrimage of faith. In addition to the story thread itself, this book gives a fascinating glimpse of life in one part of the Moslem world. This kind of information is most valuable to Christians who are concerned about understanding other cultures in order to communicate Christ to them.

In a world where communications bring us so close together, it is becoming increasingly important to understand the faiths by which others live. Christians will more and more come into contact with Islam. Thus it is important to know about that faith, about its relation to

Christianity, and about how to discuss the two intelligently. Nasser uses his own story as a springboard to approach these concerns. The reader will find here a valuable tool for entering into conversation with Moslems.

The relevance of this book is increased by recent world developments. Now as never in our lifetimes American eyes are turned toward Iran. We wish to know more about the land, its people, and its religion. Lotfi has brought these materials to our attention at a most propitious time. We pray that what he has done will be used mightily to the glory of the God who reveals himself in Christ.

Tony Ash, Ph.D.
Institute for Christian Studies
Austin, Texas

Introduction:

Why Christians Must Understand Islam

The 1978 *Encyclopaedia Britannica Book of the Year* reveals that the Moslems comprise the second largest religious group of the world. The figures indicate that 567,160,000 Moslems were spread throughout the world in 1978. James and Marti Hefley, in their well-documented book, *Arabs, Christians, Jews* (1978), indicate that over 700,000,000 Moslems inhabit the world at this time. The total figure given by *Encyclopaedia Britannica* for the largest religious group, the Christians (including the Catholic, Eastern Orthodox, and Protestant sects), stands at 983,620,900. Furthermore, according to the *World Almanac 1979*, 2,000,000 Moslems now reside in the United States.

These figures in themselves should awaken Christians to the very real problem of the rapidly spreading Islamic religion. However, additional information and figures provide yet more startling news.

First, the balance of power in the world today is obviously shifting from the Western nations to the Middle East where oil money is abundant. The Moslems of the Middle East are just as eager and zealous to spread their Islamic faith as Christians are to spread Christianity. The West, especially Great Britain and the United States, has always taken Christianity to other nations when they moved into those nations with their technology and financial aid. The Middle East groups are most assuredly doing the very same with Islam as they invest their petro-dollars in many nations. In the magazine article, "Oil Money Now Spreads Islam" (*Eternity*, September, 1979), Richard Schumaker notes that 37 Moslem countries have recently resolved to expel Christian missions from their lands and encourage the flow of Moslem missionaries to the West.

Libya has levied a 4 percent tax, which is used to promote Islam, especially on the North American continent. Furthermore, as noted by the Hefleys in *Arabs, Christians, Jews* (1978), Islam is growing in Great Britain at a rate of 10.8 percent per year and has become the second largest religious group in France. Another report by the Hefleys indicates that Islam is advancing in Italy where King Faisal of Saudi Arabia recently gave seven million dollars for a mosque to be built in Rome. Furthermore, as reported by Richard Schumaker, the parliaments of both Belgium and Austria have accepted Islam as an official religion to be taught in the schools. He also notes that 1.4 million Moslems presently reside in Germany.

How then are the Moslems progressing in their attempts

to promote Islam in the United States? In 1975, the older Black Muslim group, which had erected Temples of Islam in 70 cities, came under the leadership and control of Wallace Muhammed who had studied in Cairo, Egypt. He advocated that Islam is not racial and changed the name of the United States group to the Bilalians in honor of Bilal, the first black convert to Islam. Soon after he had renamed the group, Wallace Muhammed received 26 million dollars from various oil-rich nations to build a spectacular mosque in Chicago, Illinois. Furthermore, in 1977, 1300 Americans made the sacred *hadj* (Holy Pilgrimage) to Mecca. Obviously Moslems are becoming more and more successful with conversions, even in "Christian" America.

The United States has only recently begun to realize the religious impact of the Middle Eastern oil money. It was not until 1978 that *Eternity*, an influential American religious monthly magazine, published as a leading article, "The Muslims Are Coming . . . Is That a Mosque in Your Neighborhood?" This article suggested that about 2,000,000 Moslems now live on the North American continent. As noted earlier, the *World Almanac 1979* shows the same figure. The *Eternity* article further stated that the Moslems will soon have over 300 mosques in Great Britain.

Islamic books, magazines, and newspapers are now available in many stores, in newspaper and magazine stands, and in most libraries in the United States. Several recently published books which show Christianity in an unfavorable light include Dr. Muhammed Fazl-Ur-Rahman Al Ansari Al-Qaderi's *Islam and Christianity in the Modern World* (1976), Mrs. Ulfat Aziz-Us-Samad's *A Comparative Study of Christianity and Islam* (1976), and Dr. Yousuf Saleem Chishti's *What Is Christianity?* (1970). The authors of these books are all well-educated university graduates. The contents of their books demonstrate that

1

Laughter and Tears

Spring has arrived in the mountains of Iran. The little birds' breasts swell with joyful song rising through the cool mountain air. The freshness of the green grass, which carpets every slope, lifts Mohtaram's girlish spirit as the clean air gently caresses her face. The young girl's senses bring to her a keen awareness of the blooming flowers. Through the long winter months she has been looking forward to the coming of *Ordibehesht*, the month of May. Now the infinitely stretching blanket of green before her is too enticing. Mohtaram, unable to resist the temptation, reclines upon the softness of the sloe. A variety of birds, flashing the beautiful colors of their feathers with every movement, soar gracefully above her. She smiles to herself, secretly wishing that she could move with such grace and ease.

The warm earth presses Mohtaram to her as the warming sun smiles down upon the young girl. She drifts from one pleasant dream to another in her imagination. Suddenly, from afar, she hears the voice of a young man singing, breaking the magic stillness in the mountains. She listens carefully, but the distance is great, and she cannot understand the words of the beautiful, mournful melody. Swiftly she rises to her feet and runs over the hillside, giggling as she collapses in a breathless heap on the ground. The sound is clearer now; the song, sung in words of beautiful poetry, is about lost love. Cupping her hands to her mouth, Mohtaram dares to discreetly answer the lad's song with her own, which bids him to come nearer.

And so was the meeting of Mohtaram and Hassan.

Before long Hassan speaks with his father about this enchanting, bold young lady whom he has met in the mountains. Hassan's father, knowing that it is his sacred duty as a Moslem to find a suitable wife for his son, spends one week inquiring about Mohtaram and her family. Finally, Hassan and his father decide that indeed Mohtaram should be Hassan's bride.

The next day Hassan's father goes to see Mohtaram's father, a man of similar background. The two understand, without words, the purpose of this visit. Mohtaram's father is secretly delighted, for his daughter will soon be eleven years old, and many girls are betrothed even while still in the cradle. This is the beginning of what later becomes a long friendship. For several months, the two families get together to share with one another without mentioning even one word about marriage. Finally, Hassan's father takes with him one night, as his spokesman, an influential man, when he goes to visit Mohtaram's family. The evening begins as usual with the men gathering together for conversation and hot tea while the women cook dinner and chat together. This evening, when the meal is over, the spokesman for Hassan's father asks Mohtaram's father if he is willing to allow his daughter, Mohtaram, to marry the son of his friend. Mohtaram's father replies, "You should ask Mohtaram's mother." She in turn says, "You should ask my husband." This implies their approval of the marriage. It would be most unbecoming for either party to appear too eager.

Before the close of the evening, the two fathers each

agree to send a representative to a particular tea house the following week to decide upon the *mehrieh*—the sum of money the groom is willing to pay to his intended wife should he ever decide to divorce her.

The engagement months ahead are busy with preparations for the wedding. Hassan spends long hours gathering together and sorting his worldly possessions which he must elegantly display on the day of the wedding. Meanwhile, the women of Mohtaram's family sew fine clothing and quilts and collect housekeeping items for the bride-to-be. Hassan's father pays over twenty dollars for the fine cloth used in making the bride's new clothes.

Several months pass before Hassan comes to have the one short visit he is allowed to have with Mohtaram during the engagement period. He has sent many gifts to his betrothed bride, and now he longs to see her. Mohtaram's heart quickens with excitement as she hears Hassan's voice below. Her mother summons her, and the three visit over a cup of tea. Hassan tries to imagine what Mohtaram looks like behind the chador which covers all but her dark, dancing eyes. This is Hassan's last view of Mohtaram before the wedding day.

After Hassan's visit, Mohtaram and her mother return to their sewing. They are slowly and carefully making the customary red chador to serve as the wedding dress. This chador, much like others, is a large, square cloth that will completely cover Mohtaram. However, as a wedding chador, it is special; not even her eyes or hands will be exposed as with other chadors. Meanwhile, the groom's family is busily preparing a richly embroidered wedding coat for Hassan.

The time of the wedding grows nearer. Two days before the appointed date, Hassan's parents call three young men who are friends of the family to go out to the villages neighboring Mashad to invite all friends, relatives, and respectable citizens to the wedding. Off run these young men with red apples and candy. At each house, they give an apple or some candy to the family and announce, "Hossein Lotfi sends his love to you and to your family and says that the wedding is not his son's, but yours; come and bring your family." Meanwhile, Hossein himself spends one day going to the homes of the most important officials of Mashad to extend each one a personal invitation. He takes each a sheep and a large quantity of fine sweets as he extends the invitation. Each, in turn, gives him a beautiful tailor-made coat for his son.

Finally, the first day of the wedding feast dawns. The invited guests pour into the bridegroom's home for three days of feasting. Eating and dancing and music are the main attractions on this day. Hossein proudly eyes the tables laden with food. He has arranged for ten sheep and two oxen to be prepared along with huge quantities of various spicy rice dishes. Dishes of cool cucumber and yogurt salad dot the table, too. Hossein opens the wide front door of his home to signal that poor people and beggars are also welcome to celebrate the feast with the invited guests.

The many guests are subconsciously soothed by the lovely garden where they sit and eat. Bouquets of perfumed flowers slowly nod in the gentle breeze. The songs of many colorful birds in the stately green trees mingle with the song of the flutist and laughing gurgle of the garden waterfall in a joyous harmony. The golden rays of the sun mix with sparkling droplets from the waterfall to form a golden, misty halo over the garden.

Many guests spend the nights of the feasting in Hossein's large house, while others stay with nearby friends or relatives of one of the engaged couple's families. These three days are filled with joy and laughter at Hassan's home, while Mohtaram's family continues quietly with the preparations for the bride in their own home.

The night of the third day is feverish for Mohtaram, for she knows that Hassan comes for her the next day. Wild and wonderful dreams float through her girlish mind. Her heart beats rapidly with excitement in her childish breast as her dreams turn to Hassan. What is he really like? Will he love her and care for her as she loves him and hopes to care for him?

"Mohtaram, Mohtaram, *Mohtaram!*" She is startled out of her dreams into the grayness of early morning. She hurries through her morning prayers before the dawning of the sun. Soon all of her young girlfriends arrive to escort her to the public bathhouse for the ritualistic "cleansing of the bride." Two hours at the bathhouse pass too swiftly through a mist of splashing water and girlish giggles. Suddenly Mohtaram stands up and summons the others. It is almost the time when Hassan will arrive at the bathhouse with his friends. The girls hurriedly dress in their chadors and leave so that he will not see Mohtaram until the proper time.

Soon Hassan arrives at the bathhouse with his friends and spends two hours preparing himself for the afternoon. He good-naturedly listens to the jokes of his companions and smiles as he thinks that this is the day on which he will claim his bride. Yet, behind his sixteen-year-old smile lurks an uncertainty about this new experience.

After a splendid lunch and short nap, Hassan calls together thirty of the best young men of the group to go with him to claim his bride. Immediately Hossein dispatches a messenger to warn the bride and her family of the bridegroom's approach. Hassan and his friends wait a short time so that the messenger can reach the bride's house before their arrival. All the guests prepare to follow as the groom ceremoniously puts on his elaborate wedding coat.

Meanwhile, Mohtaram, with her mother's and sisters' help, has been most carefully preparing herself for the wedding day. She has colored her fingernails and toenails with red henna while her mother has brushed her hair until it glistens. As the messenger arrives, she scurries downstairs to the kitchen where her family awaits her. Her mother leads her around the oven seven times as a final farewell to her home and childhood. Mohtaram then turns and kneels down to kiss her father's feet in final gratitude for all he has done for her. He kisses her forehead in return and gives her his blessing. She hurriedly returns to her room with her mother and sisters who ceremoniously cover Mohtaram's entire body with the red wedding chador.

A crowd of guests have already arrived outside the bride's house, and many others have gathered on nearby rooftops. Mohtaram's mother and sisters carefully lead her down the stairs to the front door where her father joins them. Father on one side and mother on the other side, they lead her out into the sunny afternoon. Immediately great shouts and gunfire fill the air as the crowd rejoices. Her family places her on a beautifully decorated white horse, where she appears only as a graceful red figure. Suddenly a melancholy song from a flute fills the air, and Mohtaram, with tears of both joy and sorrow concealed under the long chador, bids her family farewell. Her parents weep, kiss her, and bless her. Hassan's father throws a generous number of copper coins on her head to show that he is both wealthy and liberal with his wealth.

A servant takes the bridle of the gentle horse and leads it toward the approaching groom while two other servants hold the bride on each side to protect her from any mishap. When they are within two feet of each other, Hassan kisses an apple, throws it upon Mohtaram's lap, and turns to ride quickly away. The men on horseback in Mohtaram's escort pursue Hassan until one catches him and brings him back to his bride. This gallant horseman is sure to receive a fine gift for his great service.

As Hassan and Mohtaram now proceed together, other rituals begin. One young lady places her small son on Mohtaram's lap. Mohtaram kisses the child and hands him several coins for good luck before returning him to his mother. Numerous people among the crowd throw raisins on the couple's heads as a wish that the bride will always be sweet natured. Others throw copper money over the couple as a wish for their prosperity. Meanwhile, the little boys in the crowd have great fun picking up the raisins and copper coins from under the horses' hooves.

The wedding couple finally reach Hassan's house. Mohtaram's escorts gently lift her from her horse while Hassan dismounts. Mohtaram and Hassan approach each other, and as they meet, members from the bride and groom's escorts place two threads, one red, for happiness, and one white, for purity, on the couple's heads. The longer threads on Hassan's head signify his absolute authority over his wife.

The wedding party enters the large Lotfi home. Soon the Qazi (judge), who will perform the marriage ceremony, arrives. The Qazi, Hassan, and Mohtaram's marriage attorney stand before several official witnesses. Hassan repeats after the Qazi: "I desire forgiveness from Allah."

The Qazi begins the ceremony by reading the four Quls from the Koran, the Moslem's holy book. These four chapters do not treat the subject of marriage, but apparently have been chosen for their brevity.

Again Hassan repeats as the Qazi says the Kalimah, or Creed:

"There is no Deity but God, and Mohammed is the Prophet of God."

"Alif lam mim. Allah! There is no god but Him, the Living, the Ever-existent One."

"He has revealed to you the Book with the truth, confirming the scriptures which preceded it, for He has already revealed the Torah and the Gospel for the guidance of men, and the distinction between right and wrong."

The Qazi then turns to Mohtaram's attorney and requests him to take the bridegroom's hand. The attorney says as he takes Hassan's hand, "Ali Afsharieh's daughter, by the agency of her attorney and by the testimony of two witnesses, has, in your marriage with her, had a dower of $10,000 settled upon her. Do you consent to it?"

Hassan answers, "With my whole heart and soul, to my marriage with this woman, as well as to the dower already settled upon her, I consent, I consent, I consent."

The Qazi raises his hands in prayer, "Oh, great Allah! Grant that mutual love may reign between this couple as it existed between Adam and Eve, Abraham and Sarah, Joseph and Zalikha, Moses and Zipporah, his highness Mohammed and 'Ayesha, and his highness Ali-al-Murtaza and Fatimatu'z-Zahra."

The ceremony ends, and the bridegroom's friends rush to embrace him and congratulate him. Immediately music fills the air and professional dancers fill the room as guests sit on richly woven carpets covering the floor. Soon the red glow of the sun begins to disappear, and at the gray of twilight, the guests gather at a richly prepared banquet. Other guests are now celebrating in the bride's home with her family. The guests, following custom, retire early on this night. As the guests begin to leave, Hassan leads his still fully veiled wife to a bedroom especially prepared for them. The marriage is consummated on this night.

The next morning begins with a Persian breakfast in both homes. Guests indulge themselves with thick bread and honey, boiled eggs, and hot tea. As always, the women serve the men before they gather together for their own meal.

Soon the bride's family and friends arrive with a trunk containing all of Mohtaram's belongings, mostly new items made by her mother and her sisters. Mohtaram throws open the trunk in front of all the guests. The crowd gazes admiringly at the contents—eight beautiful new dresses, four embroidered aprons, six beautifully sewn long skirts, three chadors, and several exquisite headdresses. Below these treasures lie handmade gifts for Hassan's family members—beautifully embroidered side-pockets, waist pockets, woolen belts, money bags, skull caps, and watch covers. Finally, at the bottom lies the best treasure of all—three necklaces made of sapphires, rubies, and diamonds, and one necklace composed of pure gold coins. The guests comment admiringly on this trunk, which is a great pride to Mohtaram's father.

The next day the guests begin to depart. Each guest congratulates the couple and presents them with a gift. The family feasting continues for one more day and then the wedding is considered officially ended in both the bride's and the groom's parents' homes.

Mohtaram proudly wears her beautiful red wedding chador for the two weeks following the wedding. By this, all know that she has very recently been married.

Forty days pass rapidly as Mohtaram stays constantly busy in her new home. These first days are most important to her as she shows her willingness and ability to serve her new husband well. On the forty-first day, she is prepared to receive her family since they are allowed the first visit to Mohtaram at this time. Mohtaram's mother brings a tray laden with sugar, deliciously prepared lamb, rice, sweet bread, yogurt, and cheeses.

As the days pass and Mohtaram has put her house in order, she and Hassan begin to look forward to having a child. Mohtaram is almost thirteen years old, which makes her ripe for child-bearing. Meanwhile, she busies herself with the usual household chores—gathering fuel, carrying water, cooking, sewing, and weaving. She takes every possible care to serve Hassan.

As she works, Mohtaram's head fills with dreams of the

An Iranian woman weaving a Persian carpet

days to come, happy days filled with the laughter of her many strong, healthy children. Often she vows to herself and to Allah, God, that she will always be mindful of any small lives entrusted to her as a gift from the Most High. She looks forward to the time when she can teach her children to pray. She will be patient while she helps them memorize much of the great Koran. She will tell her children about the glories of heaven, her desired reward when she passes from this world. Beautifully, she will tell it, describing in detail the joy of it so it will inspire her young ones to strive for the same goal. Mohtaram often daydreams about the ecstasy of heaven. She, like other Moslems, has been taught that heaven is two huge gardens, green as springtime, filled with the most magnificent flowers, each giving a delightful fragrance of its own, and fruit trees too numerous to count. In this wondrous place, enchanting and cool, far above the azure sky, the pure in heart will live forever, near two springs of crystal clear water. There lovely virgins are anxious to serve the heavenly dwellers.

Being a Moslem, Mohtaram has as a gift from her mother a prayer rug and a *sajjadah-o-mohr*, which is a combination of prayer beads and a piece of clay from the fields of the Islamic holy land, where the prophet, Mohammed, was born. Her forehead touches this piece of clay during prayer. She has 99 prayer beads, one bead for each of the 99 most beautiful names of God. As she walks about, she is careful to touch and name each bead. Her most loved possession is her Koran, the book that the Moslems believe was given to the prophet, Mohammed, under divine guidance. It records events similar to those recorded in the Old Testament of the Bible, but differs greatly with regard to the Bible's New Testament.

Each day Mohtaram and Hassan rise before sunrise to pray. They fill a basin with water. First they wash their hands and faces, then the right arms, next the left ones. Bowing their heads over the wash bowl, each places water on the part of the hair. They then wash their right feet and legs, then the left feet and legs. They continue to wash until each part of the body has been cleansed three times. When they have thoroughly cleansed their bodies, the young couple kneel on their prayer rugs, facing the East toward Mecca.

Before dawn each morning, the "criers," men on the rooftops and other high places, call out to the people of the town in a chant:

God is most great.
I bear witness that there is no god but God.
I bear witness that Mohammed is the apostle of God.
Come to prayer. Prayer is better than sleep.

Five times a day when the call to prayer is heard, the faithful stop whatever they are doing, face Mecca, and spread their prayer mats.

Mohtaram is certainly one of the stronger in the faith. Her constant heart's desire is to be pleasing to God. Carefully she fulfills each of the Five Pillars of Islam. The first is recitation of the *shohadah*, which affirms belief in God and his angels; belief in the judgment following resurrection; and belief in God's chosen messengers, beginning with Adam and concluding with Mohammed, who was the prophet inspired by Allah through the archangel, Gabriel, to write the Holy Koran.

The second pillar is prayer offered five times daily, always facing the Kaaba, which rests in Mecca. The Kaaba is a fifty-foot, gray, cube-shaped shrine which Moslems call the House of God. They believe that it was originally built by Abraham and his son, Ishmael, for the worship of God.

The third Pillar of Islam then is almsgiving, which consists of 2½ percent of one's income and savings. Happily Mohtaram opens her generous hand with much more than 2½ percent to help alleviate the suffering of the poor.

The fourth pillar which Mohtaram faithfully practices is fasting through the month of Ramadan. She knows what Mohammed has said of this special month in the Koran:

In the month of Ramadan the Koran was revealed, a book of guidance with proofs of guidance distinguishing right from wrong. Therefore, whoever of you is present in that month let him fast. . . .

Allah desires your well-being, not your discomfort. He desires you to fast the whole month so that you may magnify Him and render thanks to Him for giving you His guidance.

Each year for this one month, Mohtaram spends all day each day reciting the Koran and silently praying while abstaining from all food and drink, even water, during the daylight hours. Each evening, with the appearance of the first star, she prepares a feast and eats and drinks with her husband. They then sleep until early morning before sunrise, when they rise to wash and pray and to eat once again if they are hungry. At sunrise, the daytime fasting begins once again. Each day and night of the month, she hears and enjoys the beautiful voices of the men rising heavenward from the gardens with songs of praise to Allah.

The last Pillar of Islam practiced by Mohtaram is the pilgrimage to Mecca. Every Moslem desires above all else to make this trip at least once in his lifetime. Carefully Mohtaram is now setting aside money, looking forward to the time when she will be able to make a visit to the Holy City and walk three times around the sacred Kaaba. She prays continuously for the opportunity to make this journey soon.

Before long Mohtaram realizes that Allah has heard her prayers. She is expecting her first child. The months seem to pass so slowly, but her glowing face reveals her delight. She knows God will give her a son.

At last only a few weeks remain before the child is to be born. Mohtaram sleeps restlessly, tossing and turning as a nightmare creeps stealthily through her mind. She sees herself having a baby girl and feeling immersed in shame. She can see Hassan angrily grab the baby and take her to bury her alive as often happened in Moslem countries in the past. Mohtaram awakes screaming and crying. She is comforted as she remembers that Mohammed forbade the killing of baby daughters and that no one follows the old law which existed before Mohammed. Still, it is a shame to the family to have a daughter, especially as the first born. Her prayers this particular morning are especially fervent. "Oh, Allah, Most High, grant me a son that I might not shame my husband and myself."

At last, in the middle of one night, the time comes. Gently Mohtaram awakens her husband out of a sound sleep. They take time to pray very quickly before Hassan slips into his clothes and rushes out to bring the older ladies of the town to assist with the birth.

Minutes seem like hours as Hassan waits in the garden for news of his child. He is hardly aware of the softness of the night breeze, or the sweet smell of the flowers that fill the garden. Night creatures make strange sounds in the stillness of the yard. Hassan gazes up at the stars, then kneels to the East in prayer.

The vigil ends at last. An elderly lady, wrapped tightly in a black chador, appears in the doorway. Hassan can see only her eyes. Nervously he studies them; then a broad smile covers his face. He knows all is well by the pleasure he sees in her dark eyes. "A boy!" she announces. Hassan rushes past the midwife, knocking her against the doorpost in his haste to see his firstborn son, a beautiful, fragile lad.

There is wondrous joy in the household as family and friends come to congratulate the young couple. Constantly Mohtaram and Hassan gaze at the little child, tenderly stroking his soft cheek. How incredibly small, how handsome!

On the third day the rejoicing ends abruptly. Mohtaram, upon arising, lifts the lifeless body of her baby to her breast. Her loud cry pierces the crisp morning air. Hassan hurries to her side. The grief is unbearable for the young mother. "My baby, my baby," she cries in anguish. In vain her husband tries to comfort her. Mohtaram's body, wracked with grief, slumps to the floor. Now broken-hearted, the youthful parents must say farewell to the small boy who has been their greatest delight in life.

Friends come in to comfort the parents, telling them that death is not forever. The child is only on a journey to the heavenly place where one day he will be reunited with them. Mohtaram's mother places the baby in Mohtaram's arms and she is comforted. The burial place is a simple grave dug by friends. There is no vault, no expensive casket. The family and friends first take the small body to a special house for the cleansing of the dead. It is a simple structure, having neither doors nor windows, but two spaces left open so that the corpse might be brought in through one and carried out through the other. The floors of the washroom are made of hard earth, and the room itself contains only a fountain large enough for washing the body and a stone table where Mohtaram and Hassan wrap the small body in a white canvas-like bag. As they carry the wrapped body out, their friends and relatives accompany them to a burial ground where friends have prepared a grave. With great dignity, the family places the canvas-wrapped baby in the grave and covers it with a large, flat stone to shield the body from the earth that will fill the grave. Hassan arranges the stone carefully, taking great care to prevent any pressure on the small body, as many Moslems believe that a dead body feels pain.

As Hassan stands back from the grave, his friends begin to throw earth into the hole. Mohtaram releases great sobs and wails of anguish, and the women of her family join her. Hassan struggles to keep his manly face stern and fights back any tears.

Mohtaram and Hassan now hold open house to honor their dead son. They prepare lavish food for those who come to comfort them. Friends and relatives remain with them for three days. On the third day, all bathe and go to visit the grave before indulging in a great feast which marks the close of the mourning period. However, another feast honoring the dead child will take place seven days later, another, forty days later, and finally yet another one year later.

The days that follow are difficult for Mohtaram and Hassan. They are days filled with tears and sorrow. Only their faith sustains them.

Soon Mohtaram is cheered as her body again swells with child. Although she is delighted, fear, which she carefully conceals from her family and friends, often grips her heart. The second child is a beautiful little girl. Mohtaram is disappointed, but Hassan thoughtfully hides his own disappointment from his wife and assures her that he is pleased. He remembers his son and prays fervently that Allah will allow his daughter to live.

The news of the baby girl's birth is not particularly exciting to the men in the bazaar. The next two days are quiet, the festivities noticeably lacking. Still the couple admire their tiny daughter and privately boast to each other that she will no doubt be the most beautiful woman in the world.

Although Mohtaram can never forget her precious first child's death, this little one greatly comforts her, and again her joyous laughter rings through the house. Unfortunately, though, this joy is only short-lived. On the third day after the birth, the young couple's laughter again turns to anguish and tears, for Mohtaram awakens on this day to find her second-born dead. The day is somber; the winter rains have begun. As the cold months now pass, Mohtaram longs for the warmth of summer, hoping that it will remove the chill from her heart.

By the time of Ordibehesht, May, the heavenly month,

when nature dresses the Persian earth in the most brilliant green, Mohtaram realizes that she is again expecting a child. She and Hassan pray without ceasing, begging Allah to give them a strong baby. Again and again in the next few months, they exhort the Most High to make his face to shine upon them.

Mohtaram still goes to the market even though her body is now heavy with the child. Yet her legs are strong and the journey to the market is pleasant for her, for she has planned an enormous feast as a surprise for her husband. A man working in the market looks up and asks as she stands before him, "May I serve you, my lady?" Shyly, from behind her chador, she tells him her needs for the evening meal.

The aroma of spicy lamb greets Hassan as he enters the house. His handsome face, shining brown from working all day in the bazaar under the hot sun, is a welcome sight to Mohtaram. Although tired and heavy with child, she stands with arms crossed, waiting on her husband as he eats deliciously prepared curry rice served with lamb *horescht* (spicy lamb in a sauce) and cucumbers in yogurt. Twice she brings to her husband more of the freshly prepared, thick Persian bread. After she serves his tea, she sits wearily and eats only a small amount.

Upon retiring for the evening, Mohtaram feels the discomfort of her labor begin. How well she knows the sequence of events to come. She still has a few hours so she refrains from disturbing Hassan yet. Instead she prays to herself for the life of this third child. As the sun is about to rise in the east, Mohtaram gently awakens her husband for the morning prayers. Soon thereafter, Hassan sets out hurriedly for the village midwives.

Hopefully and fearfully, Hassan now awaits news of his third child. He recites parts of the Koran from memory and prays. Allah hears his prayers, and tears stream down

Iranian feast after the first son is born

his face as one of the midwives brings the baby to Hassan. The child is a healthy baby boy!

Normally they would begin the ritualistic celebration for the birth of a son. However, on this occasion, fear crowds out complete joy from Mohtaram and Hassan's life. For the next two days, the anxious couple remain constantly with their little son, postponing the ritualistic celebration in order to protect the child with all possible rigor from death. However, all of their human watchfulness is of little avail, and on the third day, the death angel comes for their third child. Mohtaram cannot be comforted, and Hassan himself sinks into despair.

2

Pilgrimage to Mecca

A year of gloom passes slowly for Mohtaram and Hassan. Hassan's patience in waiting for a son has grown thin. Mohtaram feels lost, ashamed, incomplete in life. Hassan, immersed in his own misery, can offer her little comfort. His thoughts shift too often to divorce, for he has this right when his wife cannot bear him a son. He has only to say three times, "I divorce thee," just as he said three times, "I consent," when he married Mohtaram. Then he is free from her.

Mohtaram is acutely aware of her husband's thoughts. The bitter disappointment that she saw on Hassan's face when they lost each of their three children haunts her day and night. She cannot understand why Allah has not blessed her. Each child's death was a complete mystery to the doctors.

Now in anguish, despair, and fear, Mohtaram quickly arranges to join a caravan going to Mecca for the *hadj*, the annual holy pilgrimage which takes place in the tenth month of each Persian year. Perhaps there, in that holy place, the great Allah will hear and answer her prayers and supplications.

Mohtaram prepays the caravan leader for use of a

camel, food, and shelter for the entire journey. Mohtaram is proud that she has saved enough money on her own to make the pilgrimage, for each person must pay his own way to Mecca if he is to receive Allah's full blessing.

The month-long journey is tiring; the hot, dusty desert is so barren, so desolate. The caravan has approximately sixty camels, each one tied to the other by rope. Women sit astride the camels, sometimes with a baby on the back, tightly secured with a strip of muslin. Others with more than one child have put a type of saddle bag across the camel, accommodating two children on each side. The camels often carry a total of six people. The men walk most of the journey. They push persistently on ahead of the lead camel.

For some on this journey, it has taken many years to accumulate enough money to make the voyage. They invest it willingly, however, in the Holy Pilgrimage, giving thanks to Allah that at last their most important goal in life has been achieved. One woman, weak and frail, suddenly falls down. Mohtaram weeps as several men stoop to pick up the limp, lifeless body. Tears mingle with dust on her youthful face as she watches the men lower the thin form, wrapped in simple white muslin, tied at both ends, into a simple hand-dug grave. She shudders at the sound of the crushing earth being shoveled into the hole. Horrible memories flood her mind, making her more desperate than ever to reach Mecca. Death is too familiar to the young woman. The caravan moves on, Mohtaram sitting on her camel, her head sunk forward on her breast, her eyes swollen from tears.

The caravan stops before sunset near a well of water. Mohtaram, covered with dust and half-blinded by the sun, thoughtfully watches as strong men erect the tents. They first struggle with the larger ones for the women and children, then with the smaller ones for the men. Meanwhile, other men release the camels so that they can rest for the evening. The people of the caravan now wash themselves and prepare for prayer. Mohtaram, feeling particularly low on this night, finds a quiet place to pray alone.

Inside each tent the dirt floor is covered with a large piece of white canvas. The women cook simple but delicious food outside over an open fire. The tired pilgrims finally sit and await the tasty stew, sweet meat, and steaming rice. Mohtaram's eyes linger on the people politely sitting either cross-legged or squatting on the floor as they wait to be served, sipping tea with noisy satisfaction. The women correct their children when they try to extend one or both legs. One young mother patiently demonstrates how to properly sit cross-legged. As the women begin to serve the men, the men pause by the tent candle and kerosene lantern lights to say, "Bless the food in the name of Allah, the Most Merciful."

After the evening meal, Mohtaram helps the other women clean the tents and prepare them for sleeping with mats. Iranians, being a social people, thoroughly enjoy each other's company before retiring for the night. The women visit with other women, while the men visit with each other. Conversation between men and women is forbidden both in public and in homes unless the communication is with immediate family members. When a male person calls on a family, not only is the wife not allowed to speak, but she dismisses herself from the men's presence unless she is serving them tea or food.

The next morning the pilgrims rise before sunrise for their prayers and press onward to Mecca. Night brings them just outside the city of Mecca. This night the people wait outside the sacred area and pray while carefully abstaining from cutting their hair or nails, hunting, arguing, or engaging in sexual relations.

The next morning before sunrise, all the pilgrims are up for morning prayers. The sunrise highlights the majestic white pillars which mark the entry into the sacred territory, a circle surrounding Mecca. As the caravan moves slowly and respectfully toward the great white pillars, and the sacred city which can be entered only by Moslems, the group becomes restless with excitement. Mohtaram leans forward on her camel in eager anticipation. Her eyes brim with tears of joy as she gazes at the men walking with faces turned upward and hands outstretched toward heaven as they chant:

> Here we come, O Allah, here we come!
> Here we come. No partner have You.
> Here we come; Praise indeed, and blessings,
>   are Yours—the Kingdom too!
> No partner have You!

In preparation for entering Mecca, the pilgrims have dressed in simple, white, cotton cloth garments called *ihram*. The men wear a two-piece white wrap with their heads bare, while the women adorn themselves in a single white cloth, with only their face and hands exposed. No one dresses in any way that indicates he has more wealth or prestige than his fellow worshiper. To Allah, all Moslems are equal.

As the pilgrims enter the Holy City, Mohtaram experiences a renewing of strength, both physical and spiritual. Joyfully and thankfully, she prepares to fulfill her lifetime duty to Islam. Her heart leaps with joy as she cleanses herself before entering the Holy Mosque. Her legs feel weak and her body trembles as she approaches the massive building. The stories she has heard during her childhood have not prepared her totally for the awe she now feels as, at last, her eyes, for the first time, fall on the Kaaba, the sacred cube-shaped shrine. She stands frozen, breathless, not hearing the voices around her.

Mohtaram's first duty is to perform the *tawaf*—to circle

the House of God seven times, counter-clockwise, in a greeting. The Kaaba, a small house in the shape of a square box, sits in the center of the open courtyard of the Sacred Mosque. It is draped sedately in a black cloth.

As the people crowd around the Kaaba, Mohtaram is completely unaware of the multitude that surrounds her. Tears stream down her face as she gazes at the simple structure. As though in a dream, she hears men chant in unison:

> Oh Lord! Grant this house greater honor,
> veneration and awe; and grant those who
> venerate it and make pilgrimage to it
> peace and forgiveness. O Lord!
> Thou art the peace. Peace is from Thee.
> So greet us on the Day of Judgment with
> the greeting of peace.

Mohtaram remembers the story of how God became displeased with idols being worshiped in the House of God, which Abraham and Ishmael were said to have dedicated to his worship. An angel was sent by God to instruct Mohammed to cleanse the Kaaba. The idols toppled upon Mohammed's command. Once again the House of God was purified and rededicated to the worship of the one God, the Most High.

Mohtaram walks, being pushed from side to side, to the east corner of the Kaaba. There she discovers the Black Stone, a rock twelve inches in diameter and inlaid with silver. The stone represents the right hand of God. It is believed by Moslems to be the only original stone remaining of those laid by Abraham and Ishmael in the building of this sacred shrine. Mohtaram eagerly touches and then presses her desert-worn lips to the hard surface, as thousands before her have done. She whispers as though speaking to Allah himself, "In the name of God; God is most great!"

It is here that Abraham and Ishmael prayed to God to raise from that area a messenger of peace, learning, and wisdom to guide the people of the world. Golden lettering on the black cover tells of the original builders. Before this Holy Shrine, Mohtaram pours out her heart to Allah, pleading with him to give her a son who will live, a son who will, she pledges, be a servant of Allah.

Mohtaram next goes to the Well of Zamzam, to drink of the rich mineral water which in earlier times had quenched the thirst of Mohammed. Gazing at the well, she remembers how Hagar, and her son, Ishmael, after having been sent away by Abraham because of the jealousy of Sarah, were alone in the desert. Soon their water supply was exhausted. Hagar grieved to see her son dying of thirst. She looked everywhere for water, but none was to be found. Hagar believed that God would not abandon them. As a reward for her faith, God showed Hagar the Well of Zamzam. Later, Abraham and his son, Ishmael, built the House of God near this well. As time went on, the city of Mecca grew up around it. Mohtaram makes seven trips between the hills of Safa and Marah, which represent Hagar's search for water.

On the eve of the ninth day, she goes with the other pilgrims to Mina, which is four miles east of Mecca. There they rest, as did the Prophet Mohammed, before the following day, at which time they stand on the Plain of Arafat, eight miles farther to the east. Custom requires the pilgrims to pray from noon until sundown. The excitement and long journey has taken its toll on Mohtaram; her body is weary, but she remains with the strongest and prays silently to Allah until night has fallen.

As Mohtaram lies down to sleep, she reflects on the fact that this is the spot where the Prophet, sitting on the back of his camel, delivered his farewell sermon. Apparently realizing that his death was at hand, Mohammed told his

companions that he had fulfilled his mission of prophethood. He died three months later in Medina at the
approximate age of sixty-two.

The arrival of the tenth day brings the celebration of the
Festival of Sacrifice, *Id al-Adha,* marking the end of the
pilgrimage. In this ceremony, a lamb is sacrificed, the
meat of which is given to the poor. This is in commemora-
tion of Ishmael's deliverance when Abraham was commanded to sacrifice him. Having his sword drawn to kill
his son, God showed him a ram to be used as a substitute.
The Bible relates that God ordered Abraham to sacrifice
his younger son, Isaac, but Moslems teach that Ishmael
was to be slain. Three times Satan tempted the boy to run
away from his father; each time Abraham restrained him.
After this test of faith, Allah provided a ram to be
sacrificed in the boy's stead. It is in this place that the
pillars, representing the forces of evil, were erected as a
reminder of Abraham's faith, as the evil one tried to tempt
the boy to escape.

Before leaving, Mohtaram once again circles the Kaaba
respectfully and has a lock of her hair clipped to show the
end of *Ihram*.

"*Allah akbar*. God is Most Great!" echoes the prayers
from the mosque as Mohtaram walks back to her camp.

With the breaking of dawn, still, windless, and serene,
the pilgrims begin the long trek homeward. Mohtaram
glances confidently over her shoulder for a last look at the
Sacred Mosque. Allah will not fail her just as he did not
fail Hagar in the desert. In her heart she knows that she
will have a son who will live, and he will be a servant of
God.

3

Allah's Servant

The midafternoon sun falls harshly on the caravan returning from Mecca. From beneath the feet of the weary travelers a soft cloud of dust rises skyward. There is silence except for the muffled thud of the animals' hoofs trudging along the sandy path and the tinkling of the bells attached to each camel's neck.

Over the horizon lies the town of Mashad, Mohtaram's hometown. Numerous houses, made of sun-dried brick, line the streets. Most of them are no more than six feet apart. The majority are two-story structures with flat, tiled roofs, providing a sleeping area under the star-filled sky. When the moon is full, families eat their suppers on the roofs. They chat with neighbors, as conversation can be easily heard, or overheard. A courtyard with iron gates surrounds each house. Inside the courtyards are beautiful flower gardens and trees of every variety. Fountains and pools provide a place to wash dishes and clothing. Everyone must remove his shoes before entering the house. Inside the house, the furnishings are sparse but elegant. Handmade carpets cover the floor, and even more beautiful ones grace the walls. An occasional cushion rests carefully placed on the floor. Oil-filled lamps and candles furnish light.

Mohtaram slips off her camel, stumbling, her legs half asleep from the long ride. She lifts her chador slightly to keep from stepping on the hem as she walks in a quickening stride.

Seeing her home in the distance, Mohtaram feels impatient. What news awaits her? Would Hassan desire to remain with her, or would he choose another wife, one who could have strong, healthy babies? She brushes tears from her eyes as she considers these things. Her steps become more rapid. The muscles of her legs ache as she strains forward in the loose sand.

Minutes pass like hours as the caravan treks onward. Soon the weary travelers approach the outskirts of Mohtaram's town. Quickly Mohtaram gathers her few belongings and says good-bye to the other travelers, who must journey yet further to their own towns.

On the road to her home, Mohtaram feels strangely alone. Her family will be expecting her on this day. Friends and neighbors are eagerly awaiting her. Mohtaram remembers her own intense desire to be in the mere presence of one returning from the great pilgrimage. What a great honor to touch a person following his or her holy experience!

Suddenly the joyful shouts of young children jar her into awareness again. Thoughtfully she gazes down the road, not seeing the passersby all around her nor hearing their warm greetings. The children running to meet her are from her own family, some of them not much younger than Mohtaram herself. Yet life has dealt cruelly with her up to this time, and at this moment, she feels years beyond these carefree youths who smother her with kisses.

After the affectionate welcome, Mohtaram, squinting against the late evening sun, strains to identify the figures in front of her home. Her heart leaps as she sees the familiar form. Yes, yes, it is Hassan! He is helping the butcher prepare the lamb that is to be slain in her honor.

At last the long journey is finished. Mohtaram stands face to face with her husband. Only the lamb, its feet bound, bleating in fright, separates them. Quickly the butcher slaughters the animal. Mohtaram instinctively draws back, grimacing, as she sees the sharp knife drawn across the lamb's throat. Slowly the ground turns crimson. Although sacrificing a lamb in this manner is customary to honor a person returning from the pilgrimage, or to make a special guest feel particularly welcome, Mohtaram has always felt overwhelming pity for the poor, helpless creatures. Hassan extends his hand to Mohtaram, and she leaps over the freshly shed blood to her waiting loved ones.

The welcome look in Hassan's eyes relieves her mind. Once again her prayers have been answered. The joyful celebration gets underway. The lamb is dressed, the meat cooked. For his service, the butcher keeps a small amount of the meat, the head, and the skin.

Inside the home relatives and friends form small groups. The women visit together, the men gather in another place, and the children in still another, where they play with dolls, marbles, and homemade toys of every sort. Everyone enjoys the whole-hearted hospitality which fills the house.

Mohtaram's life returns to normal. Months pass. Winter, bitterly cold with bone-chilling rains, has arrived once again. Mohtaram places a table over the oven and spreads a large carpet, which drapes to the floor, on top. She and Hassan sit on the matting, placing their bodies under the carpet, their legs extended toward the oven. On extremely cold nights, they sleep by the fire.

Each day in the normal routine of life, Mohtaram arises before dawn and prepares food for her husband. While he eats, she stands by his side, ready to serve him. When Hassan has finished, she pours water over his hands. She eats her meal alone and takes care that her husband does not see her mouth move as she eats. A Moslem woman never exposes her mouth when she is eating, not even to her husband.

The days pass on until once again agonizing anxiety, so familiar by now to the young couple, springs up. Mohtaram is expecting her fourth child. The baby is due to be born in July, late spring. Mohtaram prays fervently. She remembers the joyful voices on her wedding day as her family and friends expressed their good wishes for the couple, "May your wedded life be long and peaceful with many sons and no daughters." Though she tries to be cheerful, fear for the life of this fourth child combined with Hassan's previous threats of divorce if it is not a healthy son weighs down Mohtaram's mind as heavily as the child weighs down her body. Often she recites to herself a passage of comfort from the Holy Koran:

Have We not lifted up your heart and relieved
you of the burden which weighed down on your
back? Have We not given you high renown?
Every hardship is followed by ease. When your
task is ended, resume your toil, and seek your
Lord with all fervour.

"Oh, great Allah, Most High, Exalted One," she prays. "Grant me, please, this ease after three hardships now. Have mercy, oh, Allah, on me, your poor, miserable servant."

The time creeps by. Mohtaram's friend gives birth to a beautiful baby girl. Happy about the occasion, Mohtaram prepares food, carefully packing it in a basket for the family. Upon her arrival, she finds the mother weeping hysterically. The woman's husband sits dolefully puffing his pipe. He is openly angry with his wife. They both ignore the helpless baby, except for feeding her. Mohtaram feels compassion for the little child. Carefully she lifts her from the cradle and soothes her. She thoughtfully comforts the mother, telling her that there will be other children, and certainly boys.

On the first day of July, Hassan and Mohtaram once again prepare for a birth. Shortly after the midwives enter the house, Hassan hears a small cry. He is breathless; lines etch his handsome face. He stands rigid, apprehension wracking his body.

Again Allah has heard their many prayers. A boy! The head maidservant of the household proudly places the newborn child in his father's arms.

Like his brothers before him, the child is very small. Both Mohtaram and Hassan are frantic with worry. They allow no one to see him for fear that he might die. Because of their Moslem superstition, they are careful not to dress their child in such a way that he might appear too handsome. They fear that the evil eye might be attracted to him and bring him great harm.

Mohtaram does everything in her power to make her son comfortable. She rocks him and sings sweetly in his ears, saying over and over again, "He is my son, a precious gift from Allah. He is Allah's servant."

On the third day after the baby's birth, Mohtaram awakens in a fright. She rushes to the baby's crib. The tiny figure sleeps restlessly. Though his face is hot and flushed, he still lives. Mohtaram sends her husband for the best doctors in the town. The young couple pace nervously as the doctors consult with each other.

Darkness falls over the town and only the weak crying of the three-day-old infant breaks the grave silence of the household. Finally, late into the night, the doctors call Hassan aside. "We are sorry," they all say, "but your son has little chance to live. We cannot say what his illness is. It is quite a mystery." One by one, they solemnly leave. Mohtaram understands the situation immediately, and she barely hears Hassan as he tells her what the doctors have said. Still weak from childbirth, she kneels facing the east in prayer until her body collapses on top of the prayer rug. Hassan, himself weak and weary, struggles as he picks up his wife's limp body and carries her to bed.

The baby's weak cry awakens Mohtaram before midnight. Gently she reaches down into the homemade crib and brings the baby close to her. "Oh, Allah, please be merciful," she pleadingly whispers. "Let my son live this time." Tears stream down her delicate cheekbones.

As Mohtaram cuddles her baby to her, she understands that he is growing weaker with each passing minute. In despair, she calls Hassan and requests him to come and pray with her. Gently she lifts their son from his crib and places him on a mattress on the floor with his head facing Mecca. They place a Holy Koran behind his head. Mohtaram and Hassan kneel down to the east in prayer. The candlelight of the house casts an eerie glow over the three figures. In this special, almost magical time of prayer and pleading, Mohtaram and Hassan pledge their son's life to Allah if only the boy is allowed to live. "Allah, Allah, hear us and be merciful to us, Your faithful and humble servants. Grant us our son's life, and we will make him all Yours. We will teach him to be Thy faithful servant dedicated in service to You, Most High." Almost as in a fever, they pray unceasingly until the thick dark of the late night hours overcomes the waning candlelight.

Suddenly the baby stirs, and the young couple see that the fever has broken. Midnight is just passing, and the fourth day after the child's birth is beginning. He is safe. The child rests comfortably now. "Oh, Allah, Most High, Most Merciful," they pray over and over again. Mohtaram lifts the child up gently and holds him above her head. "This is Allah's servant. Allah, this child is bound to your service for all his life. Praise be to Allah, the Most Compassionate, Most Merciful."

Amidst tears and smiles of joy, Mohtaram and Hassan

stand together. They tuck their small son into the crib and look joyfully into each other's eyes.

Having survived the third day, the baby is surrounded by tremendous excitement in the Lotfi household. Happily, Mohtaram and Hassan proclaim that their son is indeed a special child. As Moslems, they have many intriguing superstitions and traditions. Those aware of the previous family tragedies willingly accept the birth and survival of this child as phenomenal, an occurrence directly related to Mohtaram's visit to Mecca, and her plea to Allah to give her a son whom she would dedicate as a servant to him. Therefore, Nasser's birth and the events in his life, whether usual or extraordinary, are associated with the legend of Mohtaram's commitment to Allah during her pilgrimage to Mecca.

On the eighth day, the day of Moslem circumcision, Hassan, his brother (the town Mollah), and several other religious men gather to celebrate the occasion. Hassan decides that the Mollah at the head of the table will select the child's name. The honored Mollah, following many prayers, takes the Koran and opens it at will. His eyes fall upon the name, Nasser, which in Arabic means "helper." This more completely convinces all present at the gathering that the child has truly been selected to be a servant of God, a special person with an extraordinary mission. The Mollah now pierces the young child's right ear and places a golden ring in it to signify to all people his unique relationship with Allah.

As the official ceremony ends, the women of the house serve the men delicious foods of every kind. Following the feast, the men smoke the *ghalian* (water pipe). A coal from the root of a vine is placed in the pipe. The smoke is drawn through the water into the lower bowl, and finally inhaled through a short stem of wood held between the teeth.

As Nasser grows older, he accompanies his parents on shopping trips and social visits. People who notice the ring in the boy's ear are eager to touch him or kiss him. They consider it an honor to be close to one dedicated to the service of God.

Before Nasser lives even a year, he has his first of many brushes with death. As a rather active baby, and quite accomplished at crawling, he often maneuvers his way into the garden where his mother does her daily chores. One day, while Mohtaram is washing dishes in the pool near the house, Nasser crawls over to the well, a tremendously deep hole containing about five feet of water. Attached above it is an apparatus with a rope and a bucket so that water can be drawn from below.

Suddenly Mohtaram glances toward her son as he sits dangerously near the edge of the surface of the shaft, busily dropping small stones into the water below. He laughs in delight at the splashing sound. Quickly she runs to her baby and grabs him as she places a board over the ground level mouth of the well. She returns to her chores and begins to sing. Being a curious little fellow, Nasser scoots himself on top of the cover and sits to one side on it so that the board tips and sends him splashing into the deep, dark hole.

Mohtaram screams for the servant to get help as she herself, without hesitation, plunges into the well to rescue her precious son. Because she is not very tall, the water almost covers her. Once on her feet, she finds Nasser sitting on a rock ledge slightly above the water.

Other rescuers finally arrive and hastily drop a rope down into the well. Mohtaram, holding her son under one arm, uses her other hand to secure the rope around herself, and the rescue team hoists the two to safety. Nasser has escaped with no injuries, again convincing people that Allah favors this special child.

During the hot summers, the young boy sleeps on the roof of his two-story home with his parents. When they awake in the morning, Nasser is nowhere to be found. Terrified, Hassan runs outside expecting to find his beloved son dead on the courtyard below. Instead he finds the child quite unharmed, nestled contentedly in the shrubbery beneath the balcony. Mohtaram, who by Islamic tradition bears the total responsibility for the safety of her child, gives a thousand thanks to Allah for protecting her son.

Five years pass quickly while Mohtaram and Hassan share great happiness in the birth of yet another healthy son, Mansour, and two healthy daughters, Monir and Nayer. Nasser is five years old now, and not forgetting their promise to Allah, Mohtaram and Hassan place their eldest living son in the *maktab*, a holy school for boys, in Meshed. Nasser begins his training to become a *mollah*, an Islamic religious leader. In addition to paying a good tuition for their son, Mohtaram prepares each day special food for the teaching Mollah and his assistants.

Six hours every day for two long years, Nasser sits with other young boys before the awesome, bearded Mollah and his helpers. Each boy must learn to recite the Koran in perfect Arabic. Mistakes are rewarded with a sound knock from a switch fashioned out of a pomegranate tree branch. Armloads of such switches sit in a large jar awaiting the Mollah's convenience.

Being somewhat self-willed and rather unruly at this age, Nasser frequently encounters the Mollah's dreadful switch, which carries a furious sting. One morning, as Nasser leaves for school, he spies a small container of fuel. How wonderful to rid the mosque of those dreadful

A scene in the maktab, *a holy school for boys and girls*

switches, he thinks! He carefully conceals the liquid and later hides it outside the classroom. He waits for the Mollah to start the midday prayer. The Mollah, too, must face the East; therefore, he cannot observe Nasser. Once prayer is started, it must not be interrupted for any reason. If the prayer is broken, it is not valid and must be started over from the beginning.

As the Mollah and the students bow, touching their foreheads to the mat, Nasser quickly rushes outside, takes the container of fuel, and drenches the pomegranate switches. After lighting them, he hurries back to his place near the head of the class. Shortly thereafter, the smell of burning tree limbs fills the room. Confusion erupts. The Mollah is forced to stop his prayer. The Mollah's indignant report to Hassan not only casts shame on the family but also brings severe punishment to the mischievous boy. Hassan reprimands and spanks his son soundly. Furthermore, to Nasser's total dismay, the jar fills again immediately with the dreadful pomegranate switches.

When Nasser is ten years old, his last sister, Susi, is born, and the following year, his last brother, Massoud, is born to Mohtaram. The family is finally complete, or so everyone thinks. Yet, just after Nasser's eleventh birthday, Hassan decides to marry a second wife, Masha-Allah. For one year Hassan provides her with a house not far from the house occupied by Mohtaram and their children. During this year, he resides equally with Mohtaram and Masha-Allah.

After a year, when Hassan and Masha-Allah's marriage produces no children, upon mutual agreement, Masha-Allah moves to the house occupied by Mohtaram and her children. She shares in the responsibility of caring for all six children produced from the union between Mohtaram and Hassan. The help is a welcome relief to Mohtaram. The full family relationship is pleasant and comfortable.

The entire household, including Mohtaram, welcomes Masha-Allah and comes quickly to accept her as a member of the family. In fact, Masha-Allah and Mohtaram become quite good friends as they work side by side for the next twenty years, the life span of their mutual husband, Hassan.

Nasser himself remembers and always appreciates Masha-Allah's help during the early part of the twelfth year of his life when he became quite ill with pneumonia. This was an experience never to be forgotten by any of the family. The house overflowed with people at the time. In accordance with the instruction in the Koran, Sura 36, Nasser was placed on the mat on the floor with his head toward Mecca just as he had been placed on the third day of his birth to prevent his death. The Koran was placed beneath his head to keep the evil spirits away. The men at Nasser's side each repeated seven times, "I ask the Almighty God, who is Lord of the great throne, to give thee health." The purpose of this phrase is to grant Nasser a speedy recovery, unless it is his appointed time to die, in which case nothing can save him. The Koran teaches that the hour of death is fixed for every living creature.

The months that follow are difficult for Nasser and his family. Prayers are constantly offered on his behalf. A sweet made of butter, flour, and molasses is given to the poor as an offering. It is handed to the receiver with the greeting, "May God restore him to health."

After several months of critical illness and close attention from the physicians and family, Nasser is gradually able to eat solid foods. Slowly he gains weight and is on the way to recovery.

Mohtaram secures a lamb, which is slain as a sacrifice. The blood is sprinkled in Nasser's face. Masha-Allah prepares the meat for those who have attended the boy. Nasser himself is not allowed to partake of the meat, for it is a thanksgiving offering for his recovery. During all this time, Masha-Allah has helped and comforted Nasser as much as Mohtaram.

Word spreads throughout the town and surrounding areas. The child of Mohtaram and Hassan, who was from birth the servant of God, has again miraculously recovered.

That year, during the New Year celebration, Nasser's parents dress their son in a long robe. Mohtaram takes him to the house of widows, where Nasser spends perhaps fifteen minutes receiving honor and respect as though he is the man of the house. It is customary for widows to arrange to have a male person in their home on the eve of the New Year. This is supposed to bring good luck and blessings for the following months. The women prepare delicious foods. Out of respect to his hostesses, Nasser is required to eat in each house. By the end of the day, the very thought of food becomes repulsive to him, but he eats the last meal as though he is famished, giving great pleasure to the lady of the house.

As several months pass, Nasser's health is completely restored and his mischievous nature along with it. He is strong enough to attend school again. He finally persuades his parents to remove the earring from his ear. Nasser has reached an age when being conspicuous among his peers is a source of painful embarrassment for him. Many of his peers do not understand the significance of the earring and, upon certain occasions, tease him about it.

From the ages of five through twelve, Nasser had been dutifully studying the Koran. Several different Mollahs, from time to time, had revealed to him the story of the great Prophet of God, Mohammed. Nasser is now particularly fascinated with this Messenger of God, Mohammed. He is eager to learn even more about him so that he can become more like him.

4

Mohammed, Messenger of God

Although volumes have been written about the Prophet Mohammed, little is actually known about his early childhood. Even his exact birth date is not officially recorded. It is assumed to have been during the reign of Khusro Anushiravan. The dates assigned to his birth have ranged between A.D. 567 and A.D. 573. The most commonly accepted year is A.D. 571.

During this time the moral condition of the Arab world had deteriorated drastically. Drinking, gambling, and superstition controlled the minds of the people. Although they worshiped Allah, the Most High God, they also worshiped nature gods and idols, many times giving the latter preeminence over the heavenly God. They had erected 360 idols, one for each day of the Arab year, in an area surrounding the famous Habal, near the Sacred Temple in Mecca. The great Habal was supposed to have the power of granting rain in the people's time of need.

Ubu'l-Kassim, later to be called Mohammed, was born in Mecca, a city situated some fifty miles east of the Red Sea, in a deep, narrow pass within massive, rugged mountain ranges, which parallel the coast. He was the first and only child of young Abdullah and Amina, who belonged to the ruling Ghoreish tribe. The tribe had lost most of its wealth, and its power had diminished prior to Mohammed's birth.

Few unusual signs are said to have accompanied Mohammed's birth. However, there are many legends about his birth well-known to his faithful followers. Moslems love to tell the story about two angels removing a clot of sin from the boy's belly in early childhood, and another tale of how his mother, before she gave birth to him, saw a bright light accompanied by a voice telling her that she would bear the Lord of her people. These stories, and many more, handed down from generation to generation, are not verifiable. Moslems, when telling these legends, will usually state that God alone knows whether they are true.

Some say that when Mohammed was born, all the idols in the world fell from their pedestals. Still another story tells that when the infant opened his eyes for the first time, he looked up into the heavens and cried, *"La ilaha illa Allah, Mohammed rasul Allah!"* meaning that there is no god but Allah, and Mohammed is the Prophet of Allah. A bright star, far greater than any other, is said to have been seen by the King of Persia and his Ministers, moving in the direction of Mecca on the night Mohammed was born. The mountains heralded his arrival by dancing and singing, "There is no god but Allah!" while the trees joined in singing, "And Mohammed is his Prophet!"

History does record that Mohammed's father, Abdullah, died either before Mohammed's birth or shortly thereafter. He had departed on the annual caravan for Gaza, leaving his wife at home expecting their first child. While returning he became desperately ill. The caravan traveled on, leaving him in the home of relatives in Yathrib, later called Medina. Gradually his condition became more serious. He died and was buried by family members in that city, bequeathing to his wife, Amina, five or six camels, a small flock of goats, and a slave girl.

Amina, with the assistance of a village lady, who became a foster mother to Mohammed, loved and cared for the boy during the early, formative years. Mohammed learned the pure speech of Arabia as he lived among the Beni Saad, the mountain tribe to which his foster mother belonged.

When Mohammed was six years old, his mother took him to Medina to visit his father's grave. Halfway through their return journey, Amina became seriously ill and died. The slave girl who accompanied them took Mohammed back to Mecca and left him in the charge of his grandfather. For two years he was cherished and comforted by this elderly man.

Once again Mohammed's security was snatched away. At the tender age of eight, he saw his grandfather die. The melancholy little boy was placed in the home of his uncle, a merchant of comfortable means. This man gave guidance to Mohammed during the next few years. The child, having experienced so many difficulties, soon learned to rely on his own resources. He became a shepherd boy, and, during this time, he first developed his skills of meditation.

Even in his early childhood, Mohammed spent a great deal of time in deep reflection. The boy seemed to have an uncanny insight into people and situations. He practiced rigorous self-discipline and self-denial, characteristics that were even more pronounced in his adult life.

Periods of depression often plagued Mohammed. On occasions he had seizures which, in later times, were thought to be epilepsy. These symptoms were said to have occurred even before the death of his mother. Mohammed was not the first great leader to experience a peculiar health problem, for many of the great religious and political leaders, as well as creative geniuses throughout history, are recorded as having suffered various neuroses. Apparently these special mental or psychological peculiarities, when possessed by powerful, charismatic personalities and coupled with the capacity for original thought, make a person exceptionally capable of performing a variety of astounding feats.

As a boy, Mohammed was uneducated; he could neither read nor write, but he was said to have been quick-witted and constantly driven by an inquisitive mind. He always had a keen interest in religion and distant places.

At about age twelve Mohammed left his sheep herds and joined his uncle on a caravan journey to Syria. He later became a camel driver and for years led caravans laden with Arabia's products through the desert. The products were to be sold in Syria, Egypt, and Persia. On a few occasions these caravans had to fight to defend themselves against plundering.

Mohammed was relatively short in stature, but good-looking, with broad shoulders and beautiful black hair and beard. He was warm, considerate, and conscientious. Because of his scrupulous nature, he was greatly troubled by the evil he saw around him. Extremely honest, he was so reliable that he acquired the nickname al-Amin, "Trustworthy." People felt comfortable about entrusting their goods to him because of his high principles and genuine creditability. The sellers felt confident that the profit from their merchandise was in safe and honest hands with Mohammed.

Because of his intellectual and high moral standards, Mohammed consistently made a favorable impression on everyone with whom he came into contact. He was extremely diplomatic and persuasive in his personal life and in his business dealings. For the most part, he appeared to exercise good judgment in his decisions.

At age twenty-five, having gained an unquestionable reputation and greater self-confidence, Mohammed was employed by a salesman for a wealthy widow named Kadijah. He had remained unmarried for a longer period than most of the young men of his time, perhaps because he was poor, or maybe because of an earlier love who disappointed him. It is said that he had, at one time, asked his cousin to marry him, but she had rejected him.

It appears that Kadijah was instantly captivated by Mohammed. He also was attracted to her, and most likely flattered that such a prominent, wealthy lady desired to be his wife. She had been married twice before and had several children. She was forty years old, but youthful and beautiful. Kadijah and Mohammed were married shortly after being introduced, and Mohammed became one of the richest merchants of Mecca with prospects of a splendid future. He quickly acquired a status of great importance and respect. Kadijah not only gave him material wealth, but she also gave him love, companionship, and understanding. He had no other wives until after Kadijah's death. Some years later, over a period of several years, he took ten wives, his favorite being Aisha, the daughter of his close friend, Abu Bakr.

Kadijah was the most stabilizing force in Mohammed's life, as she encouraged his great interest in religion. During their marriage, she bore him four daughters. Three sons were also born to this union, but all of the male infants died at an early age. Mohammed was said to have adopted his young cousin and a male slave who was given to him as a gift. Throughout his life, he never had a male heir, which was a source of ridicule and personal disappointment to him.

Although Mohammed appeared to have everything else one could desire, he had an extremely restless and contemplative personality. Though he could soar to the heights of joy one moment, he would plunge to the depths of gloom the next. He had wealth, a beautiful, respectable wife, prestige, and a considerable amount of power. His daughters grew up to marry prominent men. Even though he was handsome and admired by many for his wisdom and stability, he was simply not content with the way things were.

Mohammed was always looking beyond, searching for a more perfect way. He was constantly preoccupied with religious, intellectual, and moral issues. His complex personality will forever remain a mystery. Most likely he often found himself in a hopeless state of confusion and despair while puzzling over the ambiguous illusions of life that haunted him.

After his marriage to Kadijah, Mohammed spent a great deal of time in meditation. He often went into the desert alone. In this solitude, he pondered the teachings he had heard regarding the Jews and Christians. In previous years, he had listened carefully as these people had talked about the same God, Allah, who was worshiped by his own people. Many times he had heard the readings of the Bible.

Mohammed, the "Praised One," went more and more frequently into the desert. In the quietness of a cave in this barren place, some three miles from Mecca, he wept and prayed in a loud voice to Allah, the one God over all the world. He was confused and distressed by the inconsistency of so-called religious people around him. He was obsessed with the salvation of his people.

In Mohammed's fortieth year, during Ramadan, the holy month of fasting, he had his first vision and heard a messenger from God speak to him. During this vision, according to the believers, the angel Gabriel told Mohammed, "Thou art the Messenger of God." The experience frightened Mohammed. He shook with fear. Trembling, he fell to the ground. After he had regained his composure, he hurried home and related the event to Kadijah. She listened to him intently and believed that he had indeed been in the presence of an angel. She encouraged him to pursue his religious ideals.

On many occasions Mohammed returned to the place where the angel had first spoken to him, waiting with eager anticipation for another message from God. The second revelation came after a two-year vigil. The subsequent visions, though not as terrorizing, were extremely exhausting. On occasion, Mohammed would go into a stupor and lie motionless, while covered with perspiration even in the harsh, cold weather.

It was in this way, over a period of twenty-two years that the 78,000 words recorded in the Koran came into existence. Mohammed, being illiterate, committed the inspired communication to memory. Scribes later set down his words as instructed.

As the years passed, Mohammed, encouraged by his beloved Kadijah, decided to begin his mission work. He knew that he must be careful in his approach. It would cause a great upheaval in the city if he should suddenly announce that he was a Prophet of Allah.

In quiet meetings with his family and closest friends, he spoke of his visions and taught against the worship of idols and against the rich men using the Kaaba as a source of profit. Mohammed's teaching slowly gained momentum. Finally, having acquired a few followers, he publicly announced himself. Noise and confusion filled the city as the ruling forces in Mecca plotted a way to handle the crisis. They could not kill him; shedding blood in the Holy City was prohibited. However, Mohammed and his followers were subjected to tremendous hostility, scorn, ridicule, and even torture. Those caught outside the Holy City were often ambushed and tortured to death.

In the midst of this violent adversity, Kadijah died. Grief-stricken, defeated, and lacking the support of his late wife, Mohammed could no longer endure the pressure put upon him. He, along with a faithful few, decided to go to Taif, a city seventy miles from Mecca. Here he preached, emphasizing his stand against drinking. The city, having many grape growers and wine merchants, rose up against him, and he was driven out with stones.

Weary, but determined, Mohammed returned to Mecca. He continued to preach. He told his tales to strangers from faraway places. The prophet was a colorful speaker, eloquent and sincere. He had an incredible imagination, and in the darkened courtyards, he made his audiences shiver with awe and amazement as they listened to his picturesque stories of heaven and hell. Soon these travelers spread the word about the prophet to the east and to the west.

Eventually Mohammed met twelve pilgrims from Yathrib, a city approximately 250 miles to the north. They were receptive to his words. Upon returning home, they told others about Mohammed. Shortly, more pilgrims came from that city seeking him. He chose twelve men from this group and sent them back to Yathrib to spread his teaching of Islam. Islam, which means "submission," rests on the principle of submitting oneself wholly to Allah.

When word spread about Mohammed's new followers, the people of Mecca were enraged. Together they plotted to kill him. Mohammed, having heard of their treacherous plan, fled in the night on his favorite camel, Al Kaswa, to his friends in Yathrib, where he was received with open arms. When the assassins broke into Mohammed's house, they found his cousin sleeping in his place.

This flight to Yathrib, the city whose name was later changed to Medina, meaning "City of the Prophet," was the real beginning of Mohammed's leadership. A great desire to be the ruler of the people of Medina engulfed him. He decided to organize an army to establish his power.

Having then organized an able army, he was concerned about how he would provide food and clothing for his men. Once again he went away to meditate, troubled not only over his new followers, but also concerned about the faithful who came with him from Mecca into the city of Medina with no work or money.

Once again Mohammed received a message from the angel Gabriel. He was instructed to rob the caravans traveling from Mecca. This he did with great expertise. Having been a camel driver, he knew where the caravans would be most vulnerable. The success of his attack was attributed to Allah's guidance. It was simple for the followers to assume. Mohammed told them constantly that if they served Allah, then Allah would serve them.

The plundering continued, and the Meccans became more enraged. No longer could they travel in safety. They united and formed an army of their own. The Yathribites, having been informed of the attack ahead of time, met the Meccans, and a fierce battle ensued. Although it is generally accepted that Mohammed did not personally get into combat, it has been noted that he had the great ability to turn his troops into vicious, reckless warriors who thrived on violence to save their prophet. Mohammed's troops drove back the Meccans; the war continued until the soldiers of Mecca could fight no more.

Still Mohammed preached feverishly, spreading his religion. His lessons were simple. His followers must accept Allah, and Mohammed as his prophet. They must pray five times daily, must give to the poor, fast to bend their minds toward spiritual things, and finally, make the pilgrimage to Mecca.

Mohammed remained in Medina. His followers, whom he called Moslems, meaning "True Believers," became numerous. Three years after his flight from Mecca, he marched back into that city accompanied by ten thousand soldiers. They peacefully walked to the Kaaba where they destroyed all the idols. Mohammed instructed the army to leave the city otherwise untouched. The fearful dwellers of Mecca were astounded and pleased. Willingly they accepted the teachings of Mohammed.

In A.D. 633 Mohammed died, leaving behind him a multitude of believers. His followers chose Abu Bakr, Mohammed's closest friend, to succeed him. Abu Bakr announced to the people that the Prophet had died, but that Allah would live on forever. He admonished all to remain faithful to Islam.

These are the stories Nasser had heard for many years. As a young boy, he begged to hear more of this great prophet. He wanted to grow up to follow this great man's teachings exactly.

5

The Turning Point

One day, while playing in the courtyard, Nasser glances up to see a tall, well-built man with a ruddy complexion and reddish-blonde hair standing at the gate. His blue eyes study Nasser at play. His face is friendly, as he speaks to the boy in broken Persian and in English, a language very amusing to Nasser. Quickly Nasser runs into the house to get Mohtaram. Together they return and greet the friendly stranger, and through broken communication, gather that he has come to speak to Hassan. He appears so kind and gentle that Mohtaram feels compelled to invite him in to wait for Hassan, who will be arriving shortly for the noon meal.

Mohtaram serves the foreigner tea, along with a piece of hard sugar. Nasser stares wide-eyed as the man drops the sugar into his cup, stirring it into the tea with a pencil he has taken from his shirt pocket. What strange behavior! Who but a foreigner would put the sugar in the tea cup instead of in his mouth?

Nasser is so deeply engrossed in watching this unusual person that he does not notice his father's arrival. The man stands, introducing himself as Bob Hanks, an American engineer from Oklahoma City. Hassan sends for a friend, who has a fair command of the English language, to translate for the two men.

Mr. Hanks has been directed by prominent people in the town to seek a room in the Lotfi home. After a lengthy discussion, Hassan agrees to allow Mr. Hanks to reside with them in exchange for teaching his eldest son, Nasser, English. Nasser, understanding the agreement, delights in the idea of learning this odd, new language from the friendly stranger.

Nasser is an apt student, eager to learn and equally eager for the approval of this interesting man. After teaching him the alphabet, Mr. Hanks turns Nasser's attention to the worn red Bible he carries among his few possessions. Nasser especially likes the color of the book, and shortly he becomes familiar with many words and phrases in it. Eventually Mr. Hanks teaches Nasser to recite entire verses. Later he tells him beautiful stories about Jesus Christ, emphasizing his love for mankind. He teaches Nasser to use the dictionary for better understanding of words which are still incomprehensible to the young lad.

Nasser becomes more and more intrigued by this exceptional man who demonstrates a genuine concern for total strangers. Nasser's attachment to Mr. Hanks grows steadily, and he soon becomes like Mr. Hanks' shadow, following him everywhere. Many times Nasser follows him out of the house and watches speechlessly as Mr. Hanks takes the food that Mohtaram has served him and gives it to the poor on the street, sometimes sending Nasser back inside for a second portion. He keeps almost nothing for himself—only a very small portion which he himself must eat to live. He always saves the best portions for the poor.

One day Mohtaram sees this peculiar behavior for the first time and thinks that perhaps Mr. Hanks does not find the food appetizing. She is terribly concerned, but maintains polite silence on the matter.

Nasser, who is with Mr. Hanks almost constantly, knows that he must be hungry himself, having only an occasional portion of fruit or small piece of cheese. However, Mr. Hanks appears none the worse for his sacrifice. For Nasser, it is a beautiful and lasting example of the joy and blessings of giving.

Mohtaram, though silent, becomes more and more curious and decides to send a maid into the street with the beggars to observe and test the foreigner. Robabeh, wrapped tightly in a chador, plants herself among the dirty people on the street to watch Mr. Hanks. He arrives on schedule and is instantly surrounded by the beggars who have become accustomed to his generosity. Robabeh, looking as grotesque in her disguise as possible, eagerly reaches her hand toward him. He gives her the largest and the last portion of the remaining food on his dish. She hurries home to report the incredible incident to Mohtaram. They are both astonished. Mohtaram is impressed but still puzzled. Nevertheless, from that day forth, she secretly helps Mr. Hanks in his service to mankind by cooking larger amounts of food and heaping his plate to the top with steaming rice and spicy stew.

Nasser is delighted and honored to tag along with Mr. Hanks on his journeys into the neighboring villages. At first his mission is a mystery to Nasser. He talks with people wherever he finds them, telling them about Jesus Christ, often asking Nasser to translate parts of the story. When the people understand his message, they often attack him. He accepts their physical and verbal abuse, and to Nasser's surprise, simply turns and walks away. Nasser does not handle these incidents with the same grace and finesse. He feels compelled to fight back. Enraged by the attacks on his good friend, whom he loves, Nasser throws stones at the cruel oppressors and curses them loudly, saying such things as, "May Allah kill your children," or "May you and all who are in your house be burned." As far as Nasser is concerned, these are appropriate reactions. Cursing of this type is very common among the Moslem people.

Nasser cringes with inward pain and surprise when Mr. Hanks reprimands him for defending him in such a manner. The engineer explains to Nasser that the people's reaction to him is due to a lack of understanding. He tells Nasser stories from the Bible about the persecutions of Jesus, of his apostles, and of the early Christians and about their reactions to such situations. These offer Nasser impressive examples of forgiveness, which he will never forget.

Before long, the news of Mr. Hanks' and Nasser's endeavors reach Hassan. Feeling humiliated and betrayed, he hotly confronts Mr. Hanks. Boldly and defiantly, Nasser takes his place by Mr. Hanks, who stands calmly and respectfully before Hassan. His only answers to Hassan's accusations are open and truthful. He believes Jesus Christ to be the son of God.

Quite rapidly, through Hassan's influential friends, arrangements are made to deport Mr. Hanks for his "crime." Even though the American has been employed by various companies to do drafting, he has little money. His earnings have gone to lease land and buy a horse. He recently has begun plowing and cultivating a beautiful garden with all sorts of fruits and vegetables to give to the poor. Nevertheless, it is decided that he will be escorted to the southern border of Iran and placed aboard a ship bound for the United States.

Hassan now punishes Nasser severely for refusing to renounce Jesus Christ as Lord. He lashes Nasser's legs and feet until they ooze blood. Nasser screams piteously as Hassan unmercifully continues to beat and switch his son. Hassan believes that such punishment is small if it brings his eldest son back to the true belief, Islam. On three occasions, Hassan takes Nasser before the judge who gives the boy the opportunity to repent. Each time Nasser stubbornly refuses.

Finally, after Nasser's third refusal to repent, Hassan instructs Mohtaram to have nothing more to do with Nasser, who is no longer to be considered their son. Tearfully, Nasser goes to the door. With tears streaming down her face, Mohtaram reaches for her son's overcoat. Hassan demands that she put it back. Once again he asks his son to repent for his grave "sin." Nasser pauses, a vision coming clearly to his mind. He sees Mr. Hanks as he is leaving and hears his last words, "Remember, my little brother, if you deny Christ, He will deny you before God on the Day of Judgment." Nasser looks at his father and quietly shakes his head no for the last time. In total frustration, Hassan roughly rips the jacket from the boy's body and shoves him out the door into the snow and freezing rain. Tears sting Nasser's cold cheeks as he starts walking, frightened and alone, stumbling in the dark without knowing where he should go.

Nasser goes first to his various uncles' homes. Upon seeing the boy, each quickly shuts the door. Shivering, with hands and feet numb from the winter storm by now, Nasser makes his way to his step-aunt's house. She, too, refuses to open the door. Apparently all of his family is ashamed of him and disowns him. Nasser no longer has an earthly family.

Finally, in desperation, Nasser goes to the maid, Robabeh. She lives in a small hut, but she welcomes him with open arms and promises not to betray him. She remembers the good things that Mr. Hanks and Nasser had done for the poor.

Nasser sleeps on the floor with a worn carpet for cover. Robabeh shares with him her meager food supply, most of which are leftovers from Hassan and Mohtaram's table.

The front door of the hut does not close completely, and the cold seems unbearable at times. Paper and rags stuffed in the windows cannot keep out the driving rain and snow.

Robabeh sends Nasser to school. Often he day-dreams about the times he had gone into the mountains to pray with Mr. Hanks. When Nasser became weary in those days, Mr. Hanks would walk part of the way home with him and then return to the high place to pray until late at night. Sometimes the two traveled to solitary places where Mr. Hanks would sit reading aloud from the Bible with the sun streaming over his shoulder. Nasser had rested contentedly by his side until the daylight failed; then they would trudge home. On one occasion such as this, Nasser had found a small insect. He had proceeded to torture the little creature, and most probably would have killed it had Mr. Hanks not intervened by softly saying, "Nasser, the bug brings you no harm. You must not kill it. You must not kill anything." He taught the young lad compassion even for the helpless creatures, a philosophy very foreign to the boy.

Robabeh continues to care for Nasser. Through her, he is able to receive news of his family and is delighted to hear of Mohtaram's courageous defense of him. She tells people, "If Islam is not true, I will follow my son as a prophet." Because of her defense of her son, she loses many friends. She longs for her eldest son, but Hassan is unbending. Nasser is gone from the household for good.

Another winter begins. Nasser becomes ill with pneumonia. Robabeh's concern frightens him. She wraps him in her old clothing, trying to keep him warm, and leaves food and water within his reach while she goes to work. Nevertheless, Nasser's fever soars. He is lonely and grateful for the small cat that sleeps in his arms.

Weeks turn into months. The infection does not clear up. Robabeh does everything she can with her home remedies, which includes breathing under a chador which covers a boiling pot of water. The steam from the pot is supposed to aid his breathing. Once again Nasser becomes extremely thin, and the thought of death occurs to him. He takes out a crumpled piece of paper which contains a few sprawled lines written by Mr. Hanks. He had pressed it into Nasser's hand just before the military guards had escorted him away. Nasser did not quite understand the meaning of it at that time, but it was the only gift he had from Mr. Hanks, so he kept it with him always. Actually it was a letter introducing him as a Christian and requesting the reader to assist him in every possible way. Nasser's heart now aches with loneliness as he looks at the words written by the hand of his good friend. How he wishes he could hold his strong hand now, even if for only a moment.

The spring weather finally comes to warm Nasser's body, and with Robabeh's loving care, he begins to improve. It is good to be back in school with his friends, even though many of the children make fun of his clothes. Needless to say, the clothes are too small, often dirty, and very worn. Yet Nasser never allows his foster-mother to know how he longs for clothing like he used to have.

The following winter comes like a plague, and at this time, Robabeh develops pneumonia. She is seriously ill. Nasser does not like to leave her, but it is necessary for him to earn money to take care of her. He takes odd jobs, trying to earn enough money to pay a doctor to care for her. Thankfully, Mohtaram at least sends food to her.

Robabeh coughs throughout the long winter nights. The water in the jug at the head of her sleeping mat turns to ice. Her temperature continues to rise. She becomes delirious at times. Nasser, shaking with fright and the cold, watches as her condition steadily worsens. He restlessly dozes off and on during the nights, always checking to see if Robabeh has any needs.

One night, after midnight, Nasser hears Robabeh's weak voice. He rushes to her side and leans his ear close to her mouth. A strange noise comes from her chest as she breathes.

"Yes, Robabeh, what is it? Do you hear me?"

"Water," she weakly replies in a raspy voice.

Nasser turns to the water container only to find that the small amount of remaining water has frozen.

"Robabeh," he says, "I am going out for only a few moments to find you water. Do you hear me? Do you understand?"

The room is strangely quiet; no response comes from the sick woman. With quivering hands, Nasser fearfully pulls the heavy cover from her face. The light of the lamp falls upon her strangely gray complexion. He calls her name again and again. Finally, he forces himself to touch her. There is no heartbeat. Nasser's beloved Robabeh is dead. She will no longer suffer the poverty and hardships of this earthly life.

Outside the snow has drifted into huge banks. He will not be able to get help until morning. Nasser pensively considers her burial. He has no money, and she had no family.

Nasser weeps throughout the night. It seems an eternity before daybreak. Finally, a soft glow fills the sky. He puts on his overcoat, thrusting his hands into his pockets as he walks out. In the right pocket, he feels something strange. Drawing his hand out, he finds a sum of money almost equal to $28.00 there.

Robabeh must have known that she was going to die and put her money, which she had kept hidden in the Koran, into his pocket in a last effort to take care of him. Tenderness overwhelms Nasser as he sobs bitterly.

Composing himself, Nasser goes to a neighbor's house seeking help. They have known Robabeh for years and gladly assist him. Together they hire a carriage and take her body to the wash house for the dead. Before noon the fragile, loving foster-mother is buried. The entire service cost only 280 rials ($4.00).

Now Nasser is really alone. Reluctantly he gives Robabeh's cat to the helpful neighbors. A man passing by buys the few possessions which Robabeh had for a few rials.

As Nasser stands in the middle of the one-room hut that has been his home for several years, he feels much older than his fifteen years. This situation calls for all the courage he can muster. He knows exactly what he must do. Before Robabeh had died, he had decided that he should eventually go to the Military High School in Teheran. Now, thinks Nasser, that time has come. He catches the first bus in that direction and pays only 70 rials (about $1.00), a nominal fee for traveling almost 700 miles.

Nasser passes the examinations, is assigned to a bunk, and is given a couple of uniforms. It is all very exciting to him. He absolutely gorges himself in the mess hall; it has been almost three years since he has eaten so well!

During this period, Nasser receives letters from his mother. To his surprise, she forwards three letters from Mr. Hanks. Each contains twenty dollars. Since his military salary in the school is only two dollars a month, for the purchase of personal effects, Mr. Hank's money gifts are most welcome.

Nasser soon discovers that his main interest in the Military High School is an English course. He spends every spare minute learning the language. His goal is to master it.

Of necessity, Nasser had been quite enterprising as a young boy. He had worked at numerous small jobs. This experience now serves him well. Feeling great confidence, he applies for a job teaching English at Sina Institute, a night school not far from his high school campus. The headmaster hires him for ten rials (about 12¢) per hour. Nasser feels both lucky and wealthy.

Nasser's high school graduation motivates him to move toward his highest ambition at that time—to attend the Military Academy, the West Point of Iran. He sends in his application to the Academy in Teheran and waits impatiently for a reply. Finally it comes. His heart skips a beat as his fumbling fingers hurry to rip open the envelope. His eyes widen and waves of joy overcome his tense body as he reads, "Unconditionally accepted." Forgetting himself for the moment, Nasser tosses the letter above his head and laughs harder and longer than he has in years. He will begin his study in the Academy in two months.

Two weeks after this good news, Nasser receives a summons to appear before several of the Academy officials. Puzzled, he thoughtfully re-reads the letter and then prepares for his appearance.

Holding his body straight and tall, Nasser enters the Academy and walks without hesitation to the official's office indicated in the letter. Three uniformed men greet him roughly and invite him to sit down. Hiding his uneasiness at this less than friendly atmosphere, Nasser sits before the group.

Without wasting time or words, they point out the section of Nasser's application marked "Religious Preference." Indignantly they ask why he has written "Christian." They shout at him, saying that his action is inexcusable. After all, being Moslem is one of the prerequisites for attending the Military Academy. Politely but firmly, Nasser stands his ground and refuses to change his application. The officers eye him with contempt and order him to jail.

At the end of Nasser's first week in jail, an American advisor comes to make a routine inspection, the purpose of which is to exchange ideas and to make suggestions as to how the training program in Teheran could be improved. Normally the jail is not included in the review, so those imprisoned within are greatly surprised to see the American colonel. As he walks along the cells, he pauses to exchange a few words with the inmates. When he finally stands before Nasser's cell, he asks in broken Persian what the young man's offense has been. Nasser, eager as always to practice his language skills, replies in English. A mixture of anger and compassion fills the colonel's face as he understands the problem. A short chat with the colonel wins Nasser a friend and an ally who shortly has him released from prison.

The colonel invites Nasser to his home for dinner. As Nasser enters the beautiful home, he hears a lovely chorus of voices singing, "Holy, holy, holy, Lord God Almighty." During the entire evening, the soft religious melodies and the friendly hospitality of the American family warm Nasser's heart. The family invites him to attend church with them. Nasser accepts the invitation, and from then on, he faithfully attends each service. The colonel and his wife also instruct him from the Bible privately in their home.

Meanwhile, through the Military Academy, Nasser applies for pilot training in the United States. His application is readily accepted after various physical tests. He soon becomes one of the seventeen pilots chosen out of hundreds of applicants for overseas training.

Nasser regretfully bids the colonel and his family farewell. They have become good friends, and he will miss them. Yet, as the military plane leaves Teheran for San Antonio, Texas, Nasser's thoughts shift rapidly to the exciting days ahead. He is anxious to meet more wonderful Christians like Mr. Hanks. He hungers for fellowship with such good people. His real hope is that he may be reunited with Mr. Hanks himself, wherever he may now be.

In uniform

Ready for fligh

A montage showing Captain Lotfi in various stages of parachute training

Once he is settled in San Antonio, Nasser eagerly begins his search for the church. He takes the worn-out letter that Mr. Hanks had given him years ago. Tears fill his eyes as he leafs through the telephone directory's yellow pages. He is instantly amazed by so many different names for churches. He had expected to find simply "Churches." Nasser selects a number at random. He dials, but no one answers. Disappointed, he chooses another number, but again there is no reply. Finally, on the third try, he reaches Mr. Halbert. He is extremely cordial and invites Nasser for a visit in his home. Very soon thereafter, Mr. Halbert and his wife arrive at the base to meet Nasser.

After speaking a short while with these two, Nasser knows that they are the same kind of people as Mr. Hanks. They give unselfishly of their time, showing Nasser the same kindness and love that they show their own family members. He remembers Mr. Hanks' words, "We Christians are all one family in our Lord Jesus Christ." He now understands the meaning of these words.

Eventually Nasser is transferred to Tallahassee, Florida, for further training. Through the Halberts, he meets Mr. and Mrs. Albrighton who originally came from Tennessee. They help him to continue his Bible study, and shortly, Nasser desires to be baptized. He prays silently as he is baptized, "Oh, God, the one and true God, I *am* your slave. Use me to thy glory throughout my life. Amen."

The close comradeship Nasser now enjoys with his fellow Christians is soon snatched from him. He learns that he is to be transferred to Germany to serve on missions there for a year. The time finally comes for his departure. Tearfully he and his brethren in the church bid each other farewell. He will certainly miss their Christian companionship.

Once settled in his barracks in Germany, Nasser is anxious and excited to begin flying missions. His first missions are easy and fun. On the morning of his third mission, he awakens as usual to dress hurriedly, pauses for a few moments of silent prayer, and then proceeds to the mess hall for breakfast. He can hardly wait for his afternoon mission which is scheduled for 1400 (2:00 P.M.). As the afternoon approaches, he eagerly dresses in his flight gear and arrives on time at the plane. Glancing quickly over the body of the twin engine plane, Nasser checks to be sure that everything is ready for the take-off. He enthusiastically pulls himself into the cockpit of the craft and starts the engines without going through the pre-take-off check list. His mind is thinking about the beauty and breathlessness of the infinite blue sky and billowy clouds. How exciting it is to ride the soft clouds and become lost in the seclusion and wonder of the sky.

Nasser taxies toward the end of the landing strip and requests permission to take off. The tower clears him and seconds later, he is heading toward the east. He lets the plane go and drifts higher and higher without paying much attention to the instrument panel. In the clear weather, Nasser dreamily watches thousands of small pieces of clouds play hide and seek with each other. The tiny white cloud particles far below give the illusion of a globe of pure white snow. On and off, he checks the plane's altitude. It is suddenly over 5,000 feet when finally he checks it again. Busy with his thoughts, he has allowed the plane to move freely to the right and left as a fish swims after being released from a fish tank into a wide sea with all its wonders.

The sun shines brilliantly over the magnificent big bird, and Nasser's visibility is excellent. He glances at the speedometer and the gyro; everything is all right. Then his eyes slowly roam over the instrument panel to discover a gas gauge registering almost empty! According to the gauge he has a maximum of three minutes' flying time left. In great surprise, he thumps the gauge with his fingers. Something must be terribly wrong with it. He checks and rechecks the instruments. Chilling needles race up and down his spine. Another minute is almost gone. Even a miracle cannot save him now. "My God, my Lord," he prays, "help me, please hear my cry."

Numb with fear, Nasser turns his attention to the controls. Ignoring the icy chill of fear, he reaches toward the controls and noses down gently toward the patchwork earth below. As he struggles for control of the plunging craft, he reaches for the radio and calls the air base control tower. The tower responds immediately. Only one minute of flight time remains. According to the tower information, return to the base is impossible. An immediate emergency landing is the only option. Nasser looks down and sees a vast sea of blue water below. The tower control directs him to the north and reminds him to remain calm. They reassure him over and over, "You are doing fine. Keep on, nose down a bit more."

The plane sinks lower and lower toward the water. Within 800 feet of the blue sea, Nasser sees a beach filled with care-free sunbathers. As the airplane begins to shake, a cold sweat breaks out over Nasser's entire body. He musters all of his strength and training to keep his hands steady on the controls. The plane seems as though it may stall at any time and fall like a huge, heavy stone to the lowest depths of the sea. He sighs a deep sigh and thinks, *This must be the end!*

The voice from the control tower interrupts his thoughts. "Keep the nose down! Keep the nose down!" At that very moment, Nasser spies a rescue unit flying above him. "Thank the Lord," he whispers. "At least there is still hope." The two engines quit. Nasser sees the people on the beach below running away from the water as his dying plane heads toward them. He steers as much away from them as possible. He watches as the water seems to race toward him.

"My God, my God, here I am in Your hand. I am coming to You."

In a state of shock, Nasser realizes that his plane is not going to make it to the beach. He watches with wide eyes as the plane plunges toward the water. Just before impact, he closes his eyes in terror and throws his arms protectively over his head. He hears the sound of a tremendous splash and then nothing more.

Nasser next awakens in a military hospital. He has a variety of injuries. He cannot believe that he is still in one piece. After a week, he stabilizes enough to be flown to Wiesbaden, Germany, to await recovery sufficient to allow a final flight to Iran. During this portion of his journey, he meets a lovely and delightful flight attendant named Ingrid. She has been assigned to care for him on the trip. Nasser, most of his body wrapped in bandages, requires a great deal of gentle care.

Near the end of the trip, Nasser jokingly asks the hostess if she would marry him if he were safe and sound. She smiles and without answering, immediately turns her attention back to her chores.

Regardless of Ingrid's attempted coolness, a strong attraction between the two keeps her by Nasser's side as often as possible while he is hospitalized in Wiesbaden. Finally, the day comes that he is strong enough to be ordered back to Iran. With great regret and a strange sense of loneliness, Nasser says good-bye to Ingrid and soon finds himself in a hospital in Iran where he completes his convalescence. As he grows stronger, he becomes more and more restless. The loneliness he has experi-

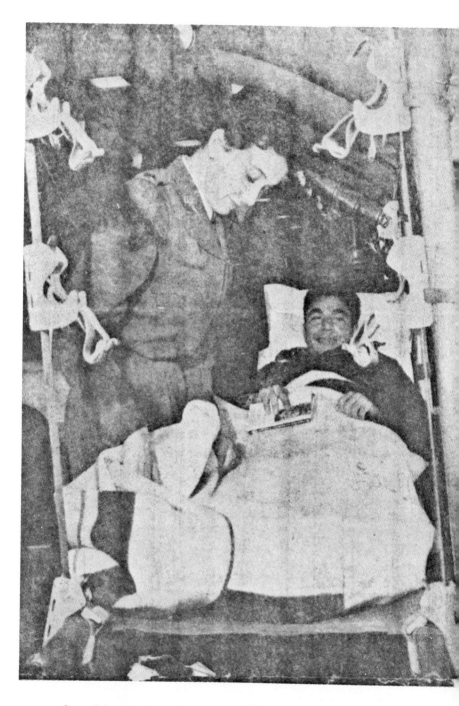

Second Lt. Nasser Lotfi, home-bound for Iran, made comfortable by Nurse DeGroat

enced upon saying farewell to Ingrid intensifies. He remembers the gentleness of her hands as they used to wrap and unwrap his bandages. And he imagines that he hears her soft, melodious laughter as she tried to cheer him up. Her lovely, angelic face appears in his every dream. Finally, he dares to send her a telegram asking her to marry him.

Several agonizing weeks go by as Nasser waits for a reply to his telegram. Meanwhile, he is discharged from the hospital. Finally, a hospital messenger brings a telegram to his barracks. Trembling with excitement, he carefully but rapidly opens it. He reads, "Yes, I will marry you. I love you. Yours, Ingrid." Nasser now feels a happiness and joy exceeding all others in his life. Even the acceptance letter from the Military Academy some years before cannot compare to this.

Immediately Nasser calls Ingrid and makes the necessary arrangements for her to come to Iran. Three months later, she arrives and they marry. They live a happy, carefree life as Nasser continues his military duties, and Ingrid works as a television fashion model.

Soon, however, Nasser realizes that Ingrid is not well. At only twenty-one years of age, she often complains of being tired. He takes her to one specialist who strongly recommends that she go to the hospital for extensive tests. He confides to Nasser that he believes Ingrid has cancer, but more tests are needed to be certain.

Two days later, Nasser takes his wife to Teheran Hospital where she is admitted for tests. Finally, after several days of tests, the doctors call him to the hospital. They are discharging Ingrid from the hospital.

"Captain Lotfi, we do not wish to leave you without any hope, but we must warn you that cancer is very serious. In fact, it is usually incurable. Please try to understand, Captain. We are only doctors, not Allah."

Nasser swallows a rising lump in his throat. What is this cancer? Why has it struck his young. beautiful Ingrid?

"Captain, excuse me. Your wife will be coming out soon. We've told her that she is very sick and must remain in bed when she feels badly. We haven't yet told her that she has cancer. We thought that you might want to tell her."

"Yes, yes, of course. Thank you, doctors."

Nasser sees Ingrid's already slender figure coming down the hospital corridor. She seems so delicate and fragile. Nasser forces his facial muscles to relax into a half smile.

"Hello, my angel. How are you feeling?"

"Not too well, darling. They say I'm very sick, but they don't seem to know the exact problem. I'm supposed to rest a lot."

"Yes, yes, I know." Nasser responds. "Well, let's go home. You've had a tiring time with all these hospital tests. I'm sure you'll feel better soon."

Shortly after, Nasser arranges for Ingrid and him to travel to Germany and Austria. Secretly he is hoping to find a doctor who can help cure her cancer. Meanwhile, he maintains a normal, calm appearance. Even Ingrid is unaware of the constant gnawing pain which came with the news that his wife is dying.

Two days after their arrival in Germany, Nasser takes Ingrid to a medical specialist. He informs Nasser that the cancer has already advanced quite far. He advises Nasser to explain to Ingrid her illness and to begin preparing her for the inevitable—death within six to eight months.

Tears sting Nasser's eyelids. He fights for control as small droplets roll slowly down his cheeks. He sits outside the doctor's office in a cheerfully decorated reception room waiting for Ingrid to come out. As she walks out toward him, he notices for the first time in months how extremely thin she has grown. This time, he is unable to give her even half a smile. He tries to be cheerful, but she easily senses that the situation is more than she has understood in the past. She grabs his arm.

"Nasser, Nasser, please tell me what's happening to me. I'm dying, aren't I?"

"No, no, my darling, my Ingrid. Let us go to the hotel and talk. I'll tell you everything there."

Nasser hails a passing taxi. They ride in complete silence to the hotel. Nasser is thinking how to tell Ingrid. She already seems to know, but even so, facing death as an undeniable reality is hard to do. How *does* one tell his beloved wife that she will die within six months?

Still silent, they enter their small hotel room. Ingrid slumps into the bed. She looks fifty years old rather than twenty-two.

"Nasser, are you going to tell me what the doctor said?"

"Yes, my love. I don't know how to tell you how sick you are. Oh, honey, I can only say it as it is. You are dying from this dreadful disease, cancer."

A great sob escapes Ingrid's throat. "Oh, no. I knew something was seriously wrong with me. I've lost five kilos in the past six weeks. But this . . . never this! Cancer!"

Her voice breaks up as tears stream down both her cheeks and Nasser's. Instinctively he sits by her and cuddles her in his arms. He tries to comfort and reassure her.

"My darling Ingrid, please don't cry. God is with us even until the end of time. Have faith in our Lord."

The days begin to pass far too rapidly. Each day Nasser watches Ingrid grow even paler and less energetic. He comforts his wife each night by telling her that each dark, long night ends in a beautiful sunrise. Sometimes, he wants to pretend that the whole situation is not real, but rather is a mere nightmare.

After the second month, visits to the doctor become

much more frequent until finally, Ingrid is confined to the hospital. Nasser is by her side as much as possible. He watches her once strong body progressively shrivel into a thin skeleton of flesh and bones. Her once bright, shining eyes now appear only as deep, dull hollows.

Nasser spends many sleepless nights by his wife's hospital bed. He eats very little. The gnawing pain grows worse. Already he feels a great sense of loss and loneliness.

Finally, the day comes that the doctor calls Nasser to the hospital for his final visit with his beloved Ingrid. He murmurs under his breath, "Nothing that is truly precious lasts long enough in this earthly life. Everything has an end." He slips into his car seat and rushes toward the hospital. It is quite cold; snow blankets the road. The steering wheel feels light and sensitive on the slippery surface. Finally he sees the hospital and slowly turns into the parking lot. He shuts off the ignition and heaves a great sigh.

Upon reaching the hospital corridor, Nasser finds his mother-in-law weeping and his father-in-law feebly attempting to comfort her. As he hugs his mother-in-law, his father-in-law understandingly pats him on the shoulder without a word. The silence communicates more than any words could.

The doctor beckons Nasser to him and clearly gestures to him that he has three minutes to be with Ingrid.

"Here I am, honey. How do you feel?" Nasser forces himself to be calm. He swallows the rising lump in his throat as he looks down at the wan, dying face of his dear wife. How beautiful she still looks to him, regardless of her ghostly appearance.

Nasser reaches for Ingrid's hand which is already out of the blanket. With much effort, she forces her limp eyelids open. He lays his face gently on hers. She whispers,

"Darling, I know that my time has come. A moment ago I bade farewell to my parents. I want you to remember me after I die. Remember the fun we had together."

A sob in her throat prevents her from saying more. Nasser, squeezing Ingrid's hand, wants to say a word, but the lump in his own throat is too great to swallow. He must be strong now, for Ingrid's sake.

"Ingrid, my love," he chokes. "You will always be the most beautiful, the most beloved woman in my life. I love you very much."

Ingrid swallows hard. "After I am gone, what will you do, my love?"

Tears stream down Nasser's cheeks. "I don't know, Ingrid. I just don't know." He watches his dying young wife's determined struggle to survive.

Nasser prays silently within himself, "Dear God, give me the power to understand Your way. Please help Ingrid. She is so young. Oh, God, please give her a chance. If that be not Thy will, however, then please help me accept this."

Pulling himself together, Nasser talks to Ingrid of their past happy experiences. He repeatedly gives her assurance that God is with her. Her eyes remain still wide open, staring at her husband. As he talks with her, a sweet smile slowly appears on her face. Suddenly the door opens and two doctors rush in for a hurried examination.

"We are very sorry, Captain. It is over. She is gone."

Nasser stands frozen by the bed. *Something must be wrong. This must be a dream. She can't be dead. Her eyes are still open. She is looking and angelically smiling at us. Can't they see this?*

One of the doctors approaches the bed and slowly closes Ingrid's eyes. The other doctor rings the bell beside the bed three times. Almost immediately two attendants with a rolling cart arrive in the room. Nasser, though weak-kneed

with shock, continues to stand and watch as they cover
Ingrid's limp body with a sheet and lift her onto the cart.
He steps outside with them. An ambulance driver stops to
help them.

Nasser's head reels, and total blackness surrounds him
for a moment. His father-in-law reaches out to steady him.

Soon a car with several family members arrives and
picks up Nasser. They follow the ambulance as it proceeds
toward a nearby funeral home. Peering listlessly out of the
car window, Nasser sees one face after another. None of
the people on the street even notice the flashing red light
of the ambulance. Each is engrossed in his own thoughts.
However, this experience leads Nasser to think and pray
each time he passes a red-lighted ambulance.

The funeral takes place two days later. Nasser has
carefully selected a beautiful grassy green hillside ceme-
tery for the burial site of his gentle wife. Tears stream
down his face as her casket is lowered into the depths of
the earth. A loneliness that he has never before experienced grips his whole body. He stays and watches until
the last shovel of earth covers her grave. Weeping, he
places a beautiful bouquet of flowers on the grave and
kneels to pray over the freshly dug earth.

The following days pass in a hazy blur for Nasser. The
anguish he feels immobilizes his body and mind for
months. Exhausted both emotionally and physically, he
finally decides on a change of environment. He makes
plans to enter a college in Austria to study German on a
more advanced level. He throws himself into his studies,
becoming more proficient than ever in German.

Mercifully time eases the gnawing pain. For several
years, Nasser serves in Iran. Then the military com-
manders send him on various missions to Pakistan,
Afghanistan, India, Turkey, and Russia. At every opportunity, he attempts to share God's Word with the people
around him. Normally his teaching arouses a very hostile

reception, but occasionally he is encouraged by finding one who yearns to learn the truth.

Upon his return to Iran, Nasser is selected to be a member of a firing squad. He objects strenuously on the grounds that he is a Christian. His senior, enraged by the refusal of his command, orders Nasser to be imprisoned. This time they confine him in a cubicle so small that he cannot even sit down. "Oh, my God," he prays, "keep me close to Thee, and give me the strength to withstand this ordeal."

After his release, Nasser spends one day in bed on sick leave to recuperate. Upon his return to duty the next day, he learns that two of his good friends have been beheaded on a mission to capture the chief of a revolutionary tribal group. The commander requests volunteers for a subsequent mission to the same area. Nasser, being pressured by both his peers and a mixture of sadness and anger within himself, finally consents (rather than volunteers) to go along with two other men.

After being heavily armed, the three men set out in a jeep. As they near their destination, they separate and flank out in three different directions. As soon as Nasser is alone, he takes all his weapons, including the grenades, and buries them. In his heart he knows that he cannot kill anyone, not even this evil tribal chief who has executed his close friends. Weaponless now except for a prayer in his heart, Nasser sets out for the point where he has agreed to meet the other two men on the mission.

Upon arrival at the appointed area, Nasser finds himself confronted by a heavily armed man who forces Nasser to follow his orders. They walk only a short distance before arriving at the tribal chief's camp where Nasser joins his two comrades in a cell. Two long nights and days pass. On the dawn of each day, one of Nasser's comrades is taken out and shot without any trial.

On the morning of the third day, Nasser is brought

before the chief and questioned extensively because he was found unarmed. He tells the chief that he is a Christian, and therefore, he cannot kill anyone. Being a Moslem, the chief angrily orders Nasser before a firing squad. The chief's face fills with disgust. He screams and curses at Nasser while proclaiming that such a strayer from the Moslem faith should have to die twice. Nasser replies, "I haven't killed anybody. I am innocent." Again he is taken to the cell.

The night is sleepless and long for Nasser. His prayers to God are not for his life but for eternal salvation of these unbelievers. Remembering Christ's prayer for his executioners, Nasser prays, "Oh, God, take me now if Thou wilt. How I long to see Thee face to face. Yet, God, I long even more for the opportunity to convert these misguided people."

Early the next morning, a group of guards march him before a firing squad and attempt to blindfold him. Defiantly Nasser refuses the blindfold. In the crisp morning mountain air, a loud voice rings out, "Attention, mount, aim, fire!" The sound of the guns echoes through the air, as blackness engulfs Nasser. He sinks to the ground in a crumpled heap. Through a haze, he sees soldiers' faces as they untie his hands. The men have fired only blanks. Nasser has fallen from fright, not injury. He is instructed to return with his fellow officers' heads as a warning to those who might desire to come after the chief.

So many times now Nasser's life has been spared. He feels an urgency as never before to teach his people about the Lord Jesus Christ. Eventually there are a few willing students desiring to know about the true Lord. They meet in deserted places, usually in the hot sun. One day, in sweltering heat, a young boy tells Nasser and the other brethren that he knows of a waterfall nearby. Happily they decide to follow the lad. However, to their dismay, they discover that the "waterfall" is only a small trickle of water, barely enough to satisfy the thirst of one small bird. Nevertheless, there are several tree stumps and at least a moderate amount of shade. They agree to hold their meetings in this private place. All work together to carve seats out of the stumps and carefully clean the area that is to be their new worship site. Small as it is, it is a great accomplishment for them. They leave for their homes with a great sense of satisfaction.

A week later the brethren arrive at their worship site only to find it destroyed. The carefully carved out seats have been burned. Nothing but ashes remains. They are forced once again to find another private place.

Nasser now teaches more frequently and more fervently than ever before. He converts to Christianity sixty Persian Moslems for whom he feels an indescribable tenderness. He knows well the hardships that they will face as Christian converts in a Moslem land.

One Persian family in particular remains always on Nasser's mind and in his heart. This family had given up all to fill their hunger for the Lord's Word. Their neighbors in the small village taunted them daily. Finally, one day, at the time of a Moslem religious holiday, a group of men in the village set fire to this Christian family's home. The young mother was severely burned and died two days later. As though this tragedy were not enough, the family suffered even more humiliation and persecution in attempting to bury their dead. The Moslem villagers, viewing Christians as the dirtiest dirt, refused to allow her burial in the ground surrounding their village. Finally, in desperation, the family stealthily buried her with only a short Christian ceremony in the darkness of the night, hoping that no one would see them. However, to the horror of all the brethren, on the following day her husband discovered that her body had been exhumed and thrown into the wilderness where wild animals had partially devoured the corpse.

While attending Christian worship services in Teheran, Nasser meets several American families with whom he shares the burden he feels for his own people. They encourage him to go to the United States to study for missionary work. They join him in prayer and encouragement. After this the Lord opens the door for him to study at Abilene Christian College in Abilene, Texas. In 1976 he receives his M.A. degree in English and then moves to Austin, Texas, to study for his Ph.D. in Foreign Language Education at the University of Texas. During this final phase of his education, he meets and eventually marries the former Anne Marion Putnam, a native Texan, who is presently writing a dissertation for her Ph.D. in Applied Linguistics. The Lotfis are currently planning to work in Europe as evangelists for the World Hope Foundation. Part of the formal preparation for their overseas mission work has included an in-depth comparison and contrast of the Bible and the Koran. This comparison appears in the next chapter in order that others, especially those planning to enter a foreign mission field, can become more aware of the differences and similarities between the two books.

Nasser's story has been told here to acquaint Christians with the culture and mentality of the Islamic world and to show that Moslems can be converted to Christianity. The story has also served to illustrate the Moslem hatred of Christianity. Why does such a hatred exist? A look at the Koran and the typical responses of Moslems to Christian teachings provides an answer to this question.

Lotfi's mother in chadar

Lotfi's mother on horseback

6

The Koran and the Bible

Origins of the Koran and the Bible

The Koran, which contains 114 suras, or chapters, was revealed only to Mohammed, Allah's prophet. Mohammed verbally related the revelations to his followers who wrote down what he said on stone, leather, and other materials. They arranged the chapters without any regard for chronology.

The scattered written fragments of the Koran were first collected by Mohammed's immediate successor, Abu Bakr, shortly after the prophet's death. Many of Mohammed's soldiers, who had his teachings committed to memory, had been killed in battle. Zaid Ibn Thabit, a native of Medina, had acted as Mohammed's secretary. He, along with three colleagues and twelve of the Koreisch, compiled the writings in the Koran as they are presently recorded. Some of the items recorded rest entirely on the memory of these men.

Mohammed was apparently well acquainted with many of the doctrines and sacred books of both Christians and Jews. There are many passages quite similar to the text of the Bible, but there is only one direct quotation in the

Koran, Sura 21:105. "And now, since the law was given, have We written in the Psalms that 'my servants, the righteous, shall inherit the earth'" (Psalm 37:29).

More than 40 inspired writers were involved in recording God's word in the 66 books of the Bible, which contains 1189 chapters. These books of the Bible are arranged in a generally chronological order so that they can be much more easily followed.

Although the writers of the New Testament did not put it in writing until about 40 to 60 years after Jesus' death, their accounts came directly from eyewitness accounts of Jesus' life on this earth. Their accounts differ somewhat, but the most important truths do not vary at all. Obviously, the New Testament can easily withstand the test of historical authenticity.

Primary Tones of the Koran and the Bible

The Moslem religion is sadly lacking in the gentle comfort of love which permeates the hearts of Christians. Fear, not love, seems to be the motivating force in Islam. Allah is considered the supreme ruler, hearer of prayers, and compassionate, divine, forgiving Creator. Yet he is never projected as a loving Father. Fear of Allah's wrath overcomes any ideas of love.

The Bible, like the Koran, teaches submission to the will of God. However, it teaches submission through understanding love rather than through fear. Christians are instructed to do good to all men, especially those of the household of faith. Service to God out of love for him and for his Son, the Savior of the world, is stressed.

Allah Versus God

The Koran refers to Allah as the maker of the heavens and earth and all things therein. It teaches that Allah is aware of every thought, intention, and deed of mankind. Guardian angels are before and behind every soul at Allah's command. Nothing goes unseen.

"Every misfortune that comes about was first ordained by Allah. He brings every event into being" (Sura 57:22). "He afflicts those He chooses, leaves in error, or guides in the way of truth those whom He pleases" (Sura 14:3). "Those whom Allah leads astray shall be lost indeed" (Sura 42:46).

The Bible, like the Koran, teaches that God is the Creator of the heavens and the earth. Furthermore, he sees all of mankind's deeds and knows their hearts. Nothing can be kept a secret from God.

However, the Bible never teaches that God tempts any man, or leads anyone astray. Instead, God is always near at hand to strengthen believers when Satan tempts them. He afflicts no one; instead, he comforts those in affliction. Only those who reject God and his love by their own will shall be lost. Every person has the freedom to choose whether or not he will follow God.

The Origins of Satan

According to the Koran, Allah cast Satan into hell when he refused to bow to Adam. Satan was an angel until that time. When Allah ordered all angels to bow to Adam, Satan replied: "'Shall I bow to him whom You have made of clay? Do You see this being whom You have exalted above me?'" (Sura 17:61–62).

Allah, angered by Satan's arrogance and pride, answered:

"Begone!" said He. "Hell is your reward, and the reward of those who follow you. An ample reward it shall be. Rouse with your voice whomever you are able. Muster against them all your forces. Be their partner in their riches and in their offspring. Promise them what you will. (Satan promises only to deceive them.) But over my true servants you shall have no power. Your Lord will be their all-sufficient guardian" (Sura 17:65).

According to the Bible, God cast Satan into hell after he exalted himself above God. Satan was an angel until he attempted to take over God's place. The Bible speaks of Satan's fall in Isaiah 14:13–15:

But you said in your heart,
"I will ascend to heaven;
I will raise my throne above the stars of God,
And I will sit on the mount of assembly
In the recesses of the north.
I will ascend above the heights of the clouds;
I will make myself like the Most High."
Nevertheless you will be thrust down to Sheol,
To the recesses of the pit.

Adam and Eve

The Koran, like the Bible, records that Allah (God) created Adam and Eve. However, the Koran refers to the creation of mankind in this way:

We first created man from an essence of clay: then placed him, a living germ in a safe enclosure. The germ We made a clot of blood, and the clot a lump of flesh. This We fashioned into bones, then clothed the bones with flesh, thus bringing forth another creation (Sura 23:10–14).

The Bible, on the other hand, describes the creation of man as follows:

Then the Lord God formed man of dust from the ground, and breathed into his nostrils the breath of life; and man became a living being (Genesis 2:7).

An Iranian painting showing the slaying of Abel by Cain

So the Lord caused a deep sleep to fall upon the man, and he slept; then He took one of his ribs, and closed up the flesh at that place.

And the Lord God fashioned into a woman the rib which He had taken from the man, and brought her to the man.

And the man said,

"This is now bone of my bones

And flesh of my flesh;

She shall be called Woman,

Because she was taken out of Man" (Genesis 2:21–23).

The Koran differs also in its account of the fall of Adam and Eve. It states that Satan tempted both Adam and Eve and the two ate the fruit of the forbidden tree (Sura 7:17–24). The Bible, however, records that Satan tempted Eve who ate the forbidden fruit. She then tempted Adam, and he also ate the forbidden fruit (Genesis 3:4–6).

Birth of Jesus and His Role in the World

Both the Koran and the Bible relate that Jesus was born of a virgin, Mary. However, the Koran speaks of Jesus as a prophet rather than the Son of God as he is spoken of in the Bible (Sura 19:31–33 versus Matthew 3:17). Sura 19, "Mary," describes the events preceding Jesus' birth. According to the Koran, an angel appeared to Mary and told her that she would have a son by the will of Allah. It never mentions that Mary conceived the child by the Holy Spirit as mentioned in Matthew 1:20 in the Bible. Thus, Moslems do not see Jesus as the Son of God.

The Koran also clearly states that Jesus himself said he came only as a prophet. Sura 19:31–33 reads, "Whereupon he [Jesus] spoke and said: 'I am the servant of Allah. He has given me the Gospel and ordained me a prophet.'" Furthermore, Sura 19:88–92 states:

> Those who say: "The Lord of Mercy has begotten a son," preach a monstrous falsehood, at which the very heavens might crack, the earth break asunder, and the mountains crumble to dust. That they should ascribe a son to the Merciful, when it does not become Him to beget one!

These passages come into direct conflict with the Bible's record of Jesus' purpose on earth. John 12:47 records Jesus as having said, "And if anyone hears My sayings and does not keep them, I do not judge him, for I did not come to judge the world, but to save the world." Jesus was obviously much more than a prophet; he was and is the Savior of the world.

Further proof of Jesus' divine mission on earth is found in John 14:6 where Jesus said, "I am the way, and the truth, and the life; no one comes to the Father, but through Me." Thus, Jesus was the mediator between God and mankind, which had fallen away from God.

The Koran teaches that the Jews did not really crucify Jesus, but that they mistakenly killed another man who resembled Jesus. Sura 4:156 states:

> They denied the truth and uttered a monstrous falsehood against Mary. They declared: "We have put to death the Messiah Jesus the son of Mary, the apostle of Allah." They did not kill him, nor did they crucify him but they thought they did.

The Koran goes on to state that Allah lifted Jesus up to his presence.

In sharp contrast, the Bible records Jesus' crucifixion for the sins of the world. The New Testament Gospels, Matthew, Mark, and Luke, all record the events surrounding Jesus' death. All accounts agree that Jesus was tried before the Jewish Sanhedrin and then put to death on the cross by Pontius Pilate because the Jews did not believe that he was the Son of God. The Bible goes on to recount Jesus' glorious resurrection three days after his death. Matthew 28:2, 5, 6 tells how an angel of God descended to roll away the stone from Jesus' tomb. The angel then told the women who came to the tomb that Jesus had risen.

> And the angel answered and said to the women, "Do not be afraid; for I know that you are looking for Jesus who has been crucified.
> He is not here, for He is risen, just as He said. Come, see the place where He was lying" (Matthew 28:5, 6).

Thus, a sharp contrast exists between the Koranic and biblical accounts of Jesus' birth, his purpose on earth, and his death.

Mohammed and His Role on Earth

The Koran repeatedly refers to Mohammed as the apostle of Allah. It quotes Jesus as having said, "'I am sent forth to you by Allah to confirm the Torah already revealed and to give news of an apostle that will come after me whose name is Ahmed.'" "Ahmed" is another name for Mohammed and means "The Praised One" (Sura 61:6–7).

Although Mohammed never claimed to have the power to perform miracles, the Koran makes it clear that his purpose on earth was to receive divine revelation from Allah, which was later recorded in written form. Speaking of Mohammed, the Koran states:

> By the declining star, your compatriot Mohammed is not in error, nor is he deceived!
> He does not speak out of his own fancy. This is an inspired revelation. He is taught by one who is powerful and mighty Gabriel (Sura 53:1–6).

Allah sent Mohammed to be an example, a witness, a bearer of good news, and a warner. Mohammed was "one who shall call men to Allah by His leave and guide them like a shining star" (Sura 33:45). He was to spread the Koranic teachings to all.

Although Mohammed was only a mortal, he served both as an example and as a teacher. He did a great deal to alleviate the suffering of widows and orphans. Throughout the Koran he expressed the importance of generosity and fairness when dealing with families of deceased men. His words and works reflected his compassion for the poor. He taught his followers to be attentive, obedient, charitable, and kind to their parents (Sura 64:15; 46:13).

As Christ had done before, Mohammed warned of the consequences of gambling, drinking, stealing, gossiping, committing adultery, worshiping of idols, and being greedy. His strong feelings on theft are reflected in Sura 5:38, which states that a man or woman guilty of theft should have his or her hand cut off. All of these vices were prevalent during his lifetime. Mohammed's heart, which was saddened and burdened by the sinful condition of the world, led him to an increasing obsession to make the world a better place for his people.

Mohammed is mentioned repeatedly throughout the Koran. Interestingly enough, his name never appears in the Bible, even though the Moslems claim that Jesus himself referred to the coming of another, an apostle named Ahmed.

Becoming a Moslem Versus Becoming a Christian

All over the world people become Moslems by making a simple statement. According to the Koran, one needs only to repeat this creed, "There is no god but God, and Mohammed is the Prophet of God," to formally become a Moslem.

The believers of Islam themselves do not refer to the statement of belief as a creed, but rather as a "witness." Always the confession of faith is preceded by the words, "I bear witness that . . . ." This assertion is a proclamation of conviction rather than a mere affirmation of belief. It is strong and binding.

Moslems grow into adulthood taking this proclamation, or creed, for granted, for they have heard it solemnly declared many times since infancy. From the time that a baby is placed in his mother's arms, these words are softly crooned into his ears.

As early as possible, children are taught to testify to the deity of the one God, Allah, and to Mohammed, the apostle or prophet of Allah. These little ones are taught to hate and despise any and all other religious sects in the world while great pride for their own belief is instilled in their minds.

At age five children enter religious schools and are taught the Arabic alphabet. They then learn to write the ninety-nine names of God and other words from the Koran. Gradually, as they learn to read and write, they go through the entire religious book, committing much of it to memory even though they do not understand its significance.

Many young boys attend the *maktabs,* religious schools conducted by religious teachers called *Mollahs*. These schools are very strict. Often a boy's parents will tell the Mollah, "His bones are mine, but his flesh is yours. Teach him and punish him as you see fit."

The boys sit on mats and rock back and forth as they chant either parts of the Koran or prayers. When it is necessary for them to write, they kneel on the left knee and bring the right knee up to make a desk.

Being so strongly indoctrinated, Moslems receive their belief from early childhood. In most cases, this belief is never questioned. Thus, most become members of the Islamic faith at the time of puberty by merely stating the creed. It is then a simple matter to officially proclaim to the public what they have always known to be a fact.

Accounts of how the first followers, or believers, of Jesus became Christians are clearly recorded in the Bible. Acts 16 gives an account of Lydia, the seller of purple cloth, becoming a Christian. Peter preached to those who had crucified Jesus, and afterwards, 3,000 souls became believers in Jesus (Acts 2). Philip taught the Ethiopian eunuch, who believed and also became a Christian (Acts 8). The chapters of Acts recount many more such conversions.

Perhaps the best biblical passages for revealing the necessary steps in becoming a Christian are Mark 1:14, 15 and Acts 2:38. Mark 1:14, 15 states:

> And after John had been taken into custody, Jesus came into Galilee, preaching the gospel of God,
> and saying, "The time is fulfilled, and the kingdom of God is at hand; repent and believe in the gospel."

Acts 2:38 states, "And Peter said to them, 'Repent, and let each of you be baptized in the name of Jesus Christ for the forgiveness of your sins; and you shall receive the gift of the Holy Spirit.'"

In most cases, Christians do not place as strict emphasis on teaching their young children the Bible as the Moslems do in teaching the Koran. The chief aim of education in Christian nations is to teach children in secular fields. In the largest Christian nation, the United States, separation of church and state prevents religion from being taught in the public schools. Most religious education, then, comes from a few hours a week, or less, in the church and from whatever time the parents devote to the children's religious education at home. Children generally come into contact with many religions other than

Christianity at an early age. They attend school with children of varying religious backgrounds and even study about other religions in their textbooks. Thus, one who makes a decision to become a Christian takes a somewhat more thoughtful step than those who become Moslems.

Prayer, Fasting, Almsgiving, and Friendships

The Koran gives detailed instructions regarding prayer. Information outlined in this book indicates that Moslems should pray five times a day (Sura 11:14). Moslems are instructed to wash their hands and arms to the elbow, and to wipe their heads, feet, and ankles before approaching Allah in prayer. If no water is available, they should rub their hands and faces with clean sand (Sura 5:6). They must always face the east when praying. Finally, they must never shorten their prayers, not even if they are being attacked by unbelievers (Sura 4:101).

Prayer is greatly emphasized throughout the Bible. Christians are instructed to let their wishes be known to God through prayer, and in believing, they will receive (Matthew 21:22). They are also instructed to be devoted to prayer (Romans 12:12) and to pray without ceasing (1 Thessalonians 5:17). However, no specific instructions about washing before praying or praying in any certain direction are given. Primarily they are told to pray alone or with other believers and to pray without meaningless repetition (Matthew 6:5–13).

The Koran and the Bible both teach almsgiving and fasting, but the Koran instructs more strictly on fasting than the Bible does. The Koran tells Moslems to fast one month each year, the month of Ramadan. The Bible does not prescribe any particular time or times for fasting. It merely instructs those who fast to do so in secret rather than in a boastful way before others (Matthew 6:16–18).

Finally, on the topic of friendship, the Koran clearly states in several places that Moslems should not become friends with Christians and Jews (Sura 5:51; 60:13). Those who do befriend Jews and Christians incur the wrath of Allah and will endure eternal torment (Sura 5:81).

The Bible instructs Christians to love everyone, even their enemies. Christians should reach out to all people of the world with the gospel. However, the Bible also instructs them to leave the wicked who refuse to accept God's Word and who might lead them astray. Nevertheless, 1 Corinthians 7:12–15 speaks of marriage between a believer and an unbeliever. It instructs that such a marriage need not be dissolved, but that the believing partner can sanctify the unbelieving partner. However, it also says that if the unbelieving partner should depart, then the believing partner is under no bondage.

Marriage and Divorce

Under the law of Islam, a man is permitted to marry four wives as long as he can maintain equality among them (Sura 4:3). Perhaps the reasoning for this was that, during this particular time period in Medina, a much larger population of women than men existed. Often women who had lost their fathers or husbands by death were robbed by their guardians. Consequently, widows and orphans were encouraged to marry as soon as possible. However, according to the law in the Koran, a widow must not remarry until enough time had elapsed that there would be no question as to the true paternity of a future child.

The four wives a man is allowed should be virtuous and believers in the Islamic faith. If a man felt that he could not deal equitably with more than one wife, then he should marry only one woman. He should give each wife her dowry freely. His duty was to support all his wives, clothing them and giving them protection and speaking kindly to each one. In this way, men are to live chastely with their wife or wives, without fornication and without taking concubines (Sura 5:5).

Moslems are instructed not to marry idolatresses, or their daughters, unless they become believers. Furthermore, under Islam, one should not marry his mother, daughter, sister, aunt, niece, foster mother, foster sister, stepmother, mother-in-law, or stepdaughter, unless the marriage to the mother of the stepdaughter was never consummated. Furthermore, a man was forbidden to marry two sisters at the same time. Finally, the Koran instructs men not to marry any married woman except for a married woman taken as captive during a time of war (Sura 4:23–24).

According to history, Mohammed's own life style was inconsistent with the teachings of the Koran for all other believers. Mohammed explained these discrepancies between his own life and the teachings of the Koran by saying that God had granted him special privilege as a prophet (Sura 33:49). Mohammed had ten wives following the death of his first wife, Khadija. None of his wives were widows. One was the wife of his adopted son, Zeid, who divorced his wife to please the prophet. Another of his wives was the daughter of his good friend and successor, Abu Bakr. This young girl was betrothed to him at the tender age of six. Mohammed married her when she was nine years old. He also married a fifty-one-year-old kinswoman. In addition to these eleven wives, he had two concubines. One was a Jewish widow taken captive after a battle, and the other was a Coptic slave girl who was sent to him by the Roman governor of Egypt. She gave Mohammed a son, who died before age two. The Koran states that Mohammed had no living male heirs even though tradition lists four sons born to him, all of whom died at a very early age.

The Bible is strongly against polygamy. 1 Corinthians 7

is dedicated to the subject of marriage. Verse two of this chapter clearly states that each man should have his own wife and each woman should have her own husband in order to prevent immoralities. When two people marry, they become one flesh (Matthew 19:5).

According to the Bible, a man should not marry his mother, sister, or mother-in-law (Deuteronomy 27:20, 22, 23). Furthermore, a man should not marry his granddaughter, aunt, daughter-in-law, sister-in-law, or stepdaughter (Leviticus 18:8–17). Finally, a man should not marry two sisters so that they become rivals (Leviticus 18:18).

A Moslem husband may divorce his wife if he no longer finds her desirable, or if he finds another whom he wishes to marry. However, a man who wishes to divorce must put his wife away with generosity and must deal kindly with her. This means that he must give the woman her rightful dowry (Sura 4:21) and keep her until her waiting time is over (Sura 65:1). The waiting period is three months. Its purpose is to determine whether or not a woman is pregnant (Sura 65:4). If the wife is pregnant, then the husband should support her and the child until the end of their confinement (Sura 65:6).

To divorce his wife, a man must wait four months after stating three times, "I divorce thee, I divorce thee, I divorce thee." Once a man has divorced his wife, he cannot remarry her until she has married another man and been divorced by him (Sura 2:230). However, if a man divorces his wife and her waiting period has been reached, she should not be prevented from remarrying her husband if they come to an agreement (Sura 2:232).

The Bible protects the family unit very carefully by stating that a husband and wife are bound together by law until death (Romans 7:2, 3). Matthew 19:6 says of married couples: "Consequently they are no more two, but one flesh. What therefore God has joined together, let no man separate."

Divorce is a very serious matter according to the Bible. When asked why Moses allowed divorce by giving the wife a certificate of divorce, Jesus said:

> Because of your hardness of heart, Moses permitted you to divorce your wives; but from the beginning it has not been this way.
>
> And I say to you, whoever divorces his wife, except for immorality, and marries another commits adultery (Matthew 19:8, 9).

Mark 10:11, 12 not only forbids a man to divorce his wife, except for adultery, but it also forbids the wife to divorce her husband, except for adultery. If a Christian divorces, neither should remarry unless they remarry each other (1 Corinthians 7:10, 11). The Bible goes even further to state that a Christian married to an unbeliever should remain with that unbelieving mate (1 Corinthians 7:12–16). However, if an unbelieving spouse leaves the believing spouse, then the believer is not under bondage (1 Corinthians 7:15).

The End Times and the Judgment

The Koran gives detailed accounts of what will happen at the end of time. Much of the writing coincides with Bible prophecy.

According to the Koran, the Day of Judgment is fixed (Sura 78:14). Furthermore, the Hour of Doom is unknown to man. The Lord alone knows when it will come. The Moslem's duty is to warn those who fear it (Sura 79:42–45).

The Koran describes these last days in several different

suras. In Sura 99:1–8, the writers record that the earth will rock in her last great convulsion. Sura 82:1–4 states that the sky will be torn asunder, the stars will scatter, and the oceans will roll together. Furthermore, graves will be hurled about. At this time, each soul will know what it has done and what it has failed to do. Sura 81:1–21 describes the last days in this way:

> When the sun ceases to shine; when the stars fall down and the mountains are blown away; when camels big with young are left untended and the wild beasts are brought together; when the seas are set alight and men's souls are reunited; when the infant girl, buried alive, is asked for what crime she was slain; when the records of men's deeds are laid open and the heaven is stripped bare; when Hell burns fiercely and Paradise is brought near: then each soul shall know what it has done.

The Koran also reveals that on the Day of Judgment, people will forget friends and relatives and sacrifice anything to redeem themselves from the torment of that day (Sura 70:8–12). When the dread blast of the trumpet is sounded, terror will fill the hearts of all, and all eyes will stare with awe (Sura 79:5). Furthermore, when that dread blast is heard, all men will forsake their brother, father, mother, wife, and children (Sura 80:36–40).

According to the Koran, after the trumpet sounds a single blast, the sky will be torn asunder and angels will stand on all its sides. Eight of these angels will be carrying the throne of the Lord above their heads, and the judgment will begin (Sura 69:17, 18). Those who are given the Lord's book in their right hands will be the ones who have prepared themselves and who will be rewarded. Those who are given the Lord's book in their left hands are those who will be condemned to hell, for they have not given thought to Allah and his teachings (Sura 69:20–30). The Koran further states the following:

On that day there shall be downcast faces, of men broken and worn out, burnt by a scorching fire, drinking from a seething fountain. Their only food shall be bitter thorns, which will neither sustain them nor satisfy their hunger.

On that day there shall be radiant faces, of men well-pleased with their labours, in a lofty garden. There they shall hear no idle talk. A gushing fountain shall be there, and raised soft couches with goblets placed before them; silken cushions ranged in order and carpets richly spread.

The Bible describes the end times and the judgment in a similar way. It, too, states that God alone knows the day and the hour of the judgment (Mark 13:32). In the last days, the sun will darken, and the moon will not give light (Mark 13:24). Furthermore, the stars will fall, and the heavens will shake. Then, all will see Christ Jesus coming in the clouds to gather together all of the believers on earth (Mark 13:25–27). During this period, the sky will split apart and every mountain and island will be moved out of its place (Revelation 6:14).

At the final judgment, all will stand before the throne of God. Books will be opened and the dead will be judged according to their deeds. All those whose names do not appear in the Book of Life will be thrown into a lake of fire, or hell. All those whose names appear in the Book of Life will go to heaven to be with the Father (Revelation 20:12–15).

The Bible's account of the final days and judgment is much more detailed and complex than the Koranic account. Revelation gives the most detailed account found in the Bible.

Hell

The Koran describes hell as an awful place with moaning souls which wander between fire and fiercely seething waters (Sura 55:43). They will be burned with flames of fire and molten brass (Sura 55:38). Furthermore, they will be burdened with iron collars and heavy chains seventy cubits long (Sura 69:31). These souls will be friendless and eat filth for food (Sura 69:32).

The fires of hell are emphasized in several different suras. One of the more descriptive suras is Sura 77:28 which states:

> Woe on that day to the disbelievers! Begone to that Hell which you deny! Depart into the shadow that will rise high in three columns, giving neither shade nor shelter from the flames and throwing up sparks as huge as towers, as bright as yellow camels!

The hell described in the Bible is equally as frightening and horrifying. In Revelation 21:8, hell is described as "the lake that burns with fire and brimstone, which is the second death." Hell is referred to as "the eternal fire" several times in the Book of Jude. Furthermore, Matthew 25:30 describes hell as "outer darkness; in that place there shall be weeping and gnashing of teeth."

Paradise, or Heaven

In both the Koran and the Bible heaven is the place reserved for the faithful believers. The Koran describes it as a garden of delight (Sura 10:9). It is also referred to as the gardens of Eden (Sura 19:61). In heaven the dwellers hear no idle talk; they hear only the voice of peace. Their sustenance is given to them day and night (Sura 19:62).

In heaven, the righteous dwellers will be given green silk robes covered with brocade and silver bracelets. They will also receive from Allah pure ginger flavored water to drink (Sura 76:15–20). Heaven is a place of cool shades and fountains where the dwellers can feed on whatever fruits they desire (Sura 77:37). Boys graced with eternal youth will serve the righteous dwellers from silver goblets and silver dishes (Sura 76:15–19). Rivers will roll at their feet, and they will recline on soft couches (Sura 18:31, 32).

Heaven or Paradise, as spoken of in the Koran, is filled with other sensual delights as well. Houris (beautiful young virgins) with large eyes may be married in Paradise (Sura 44:51). Furthermore, the companions of the righteous dwellers will be high-bosomed maidens (Sura 78:30).

The prayer of the dwellers of Paradise will be: "Glory to You, Lord." Their greeting will be: "Peace." Their hymn will be: "Allah, Lord of the Creation" (Sura 10:10).

Heaven, as described in the Bible, does not contain such sensual delights, but focuses more on delightful service to God. Revelation has the best description of heaven. It is the crystal clear river of life coming from the throne of God and Jesus Christ. On either side of the river is the tree of life which bears twelve kinds of fruit. There is no darkness and no need for lamps or the light of the sun, for God illumines all (Revelation 22:1–5).

Jesus himself referred to heaven as Paradise. When one of the criminals who was being crucified next to Jesus asked Jesus to remember him, Jesus replied, "'Truly I say to you, today you shall be with Me in Paradise.'" Heaven is referred to throughout the Bible as God's kingdom.

Summary

While the Koran and the Bible share some similarities, they also differ on many vital issues. Both Moslems and Christians believe in their "sacred book." Both groups are sincere in their efforts to reach others. The next and final chapters of this book examine the present state of Islam in the world and bring out many important questions and answers regarding the two faiths.

7

What Moslems Say about Christianity

This chapter serves as a short but vital commentary on the more important issues concerning Christianity from the Moslem point of view. The information here provides a framework for better understanding of the intense debate contained in the next chapter.

The most important element of the Moslem view of Christianity is that the Bible lacks authenticity. The Koran is the only book of authentic revealed scripture. Moslems believe that every religious group in the world has had a divine messenger who was a human being. All of these messengers (including Jesus) taught the same message—submission to the will of God. The Moslems regard all these messengers as great prophets. However, they believe that their messenger, the Prophet Mohammed, was the last of all such messengers and that he perfected all religion and scripture in the Koranic revelation. Although Moslems believe in all revealed scripture, they follow the Koran first because they believe that it alone contains the authentic teachings given in all former scripture and because none of the former scriptures exists in original and pure form.

Some Moslems have thoroughly researched the writing

of the Christian New Testament to show that it lacks authenticity. One of their major points is that the New Testament writings were not even begun until at least 40 to 60 years after Jesus' death. In contrast, the writings of the Koran were begun at the time of the Prophet Mohammed's first revelation and ended when he died. All records of his revelations were then gathered together, compiled into one book, and checked by several followers who had committed all of the revelations to memory.

Of course, the Christian knows that even though the New Testament was written some 40 to 60 years after Jesus' death, it was written by men who relied upon eyewitness accounts of Jesus' life. It was not written before his death because people followed the oral tradition of teaching during that time period. It was only after the message began to spread to other countries that three men, Matthew, Mark, and Luke, decided to write down the eyewitness accounts of Christ's life. The accounts written by these ancient historians are just as factual and accurate as historical accounts written by such well-known men as Philo of Alexandria (30 B.C.–A.D. 45) and Plutarch (A.D. 50–120). The Gospels were originally historical accounts of Christ's life.

A second major point is that the Gospels of the New Testament were written after the early Christians had become divided into factions. Thus, Moslems believe that once they were so divided (which is against the teachings of both the Bible and the Koran), the writers of Jesus' sayings did not hesitate to tamper with earlier documents and traditions to make their writings fit their beliefs. True Moslems have never been divided as Christians have. The only division is between the Sunnites and the Shiites. Their division is based solely on a dispute as to the successor of Mohammed. However, both groups fully believe the Koran and follow its teachings.

Christians realize that the early church, at the time of the writing of the Bible, was unified. No divisions or factions existed until A.D. 325 when Constantine caused division. Furthermore, the early church existed before the Gospels were written. Thus, the church, as a unified group, provided a restraining influence on the writers of the Gospels. The church made sure that the accounts of Christ's life remained factual according to eyewitnesses.

A third major point brought up by Moslems is that manuscripts for the New Testament Gospels were written in Greek even though Jesus and his disciples preached in Israel where Hebrew and Aramaic were the predominant languages. Moslems have often quoted from J. R. Dummelow's *Commentary on the Holy Bible:*

> To begin with, the writers of the Gospels report in Greek (although they may have had some Aramaic sources) the sayings of Jesus Christ who for the most part probably spoke Aramaic. Nor is it likely that these writers or their copyists had any idea that their records would go beyond the early Churches with which they themselves were familiar. . . . Nor even in the later centuries do we find that scrupulous regard for the sacred text which marked the transmission of the Old Testament. A copyist would sometimes put in not what was in the text, but what he thought ought to be in it. He would trust a fickle memory, or he would even make the text accord with the views of the school to which he belonged. Besides this, an enormous number of copies were preserved. In addition to the versions and quotations from the early Church Fathers, nearly four thousand Greek manuscripts of the New Testament are known to exist. As a result, the variety of reading is considerable.

Moslems then note that the entire Koran was written in the Prophet Mohammed's native language, Arabic. Even today Moslems believe that only the original Arabic Koran is the authentic, uncorrupted teachings of Mohammed.

They stress that all Moslems should learn Arabic and study the Koran in that language. Translations to any other languages may corrupt the original and true book.

These Moslem arguments dismiss the fact that Greek, not the formal classical Greek of the intellectuals, but the "koine" (common) Greek, was the language of the common people and widely spoken from 300 B.C. to A.D. 330.

Next, from the Moslem viewpoint, the Bible contains irrational beliefs and indecent stories. A prime example is the story of David to whom the Bible attributes both saintliness and immorality at the same time. In contrast, the Koran is rational, scientific, and modern. It emphasizes practical ethics. Although it narrates several stories which are also found in the Bible, it leaves out all obscene and contradictory accounts of these stories.

The Moslems obviously wish to believe in a perfection of certain men in the Koran. However, historically this simply is not true. The Bible records the truth. It does not make up irrational or indecent stories, but neither does it hide what is true.

Finally, from the Moslem viewpoint, the New Testament is full of contradictions. A prime example is the conflict in the teachings of James as opposed to the teachings of Paul. In James 2:14, James wrote, "What use is it, my brethren, if a man says he has faith, but he has no works? Can that faith save him?" He further stated in James 2:24, "You see that a man is justified by works, and not by faith alone." Yet, Paul taught that one is saved by faith alone as stated in Romans 10:13: "For 'Whoever will call upon the name of the Lord will be saved.'"

However, Moslems must study the whole Bible to realize that these are, in context, statements which complement rather than contradict one another. Each writer was addressing a different audience. Placed together, they mean that one who truly has faith will demonstrate his faith through good works.

Another seeming contradiction cited by Moslems involves Jesus' words in Matthew 19:17 and Mark 10:18 and John's words in 1 John 3:5. Matthew 19:17 and Mark 10:18 read, "And He said to him, 'Why are you asking Me about what is good? There is only One who is good . . . God alone.'" The passage from 1 John, however, indicates that Jesus was not only good, but perfect. "And you know that He appeared in order to take away sins; and in Him there is no sin." If Jesus was without sin, argue the Moslems, then he must have been good. Yet, he said that he was not good. His statement in Matthew and Mark indicates, too, that he was not a part of God, but rather was inferior to God.

Yet, what seems to be contradiction here is actually a misunderstanding created by the Moslem's refusal to accept the unique nature of Christ—the divine nature and the human nature in one. When Jesus spoke of not being good as God is, he was speaking of the human part of his unique nature. Philippians 2:5–11 makes Jesus' position clear:

Have this attitude in yourselves which was also in Christ Jesus,

who, although He existed in the form of God, did not regard equality with God a thing to be grasped,

but emptied Himself, taking the form of a bond-servant, and being made in the likeness of men.

And being found in appearance as a man, He humbled Himself by becoming obedient to the point of death, even death on a cross.

Therefore also God highly exalted Him, and bestowed on Him the name which is above every name,

that at the name of Jesus every knee should bow, of those who are in heaven, and on earth, and under the earth,

and that every tongue should confess that Jesus Christ is Lord, to the glory of God the Father.

Yet, in John 8:58, Jesus clearly stated, "'Truly, truly, I say to you, before Abraham was born, I AM.'" The "I AM" here obviously refers to God who said in Exodus 3:14, "I AM WHO I AM." Thus, in these passages, the spiritual nature of Jesus identifies itself as equal to God.

Besides attacking the Bible's credibility and authenticity, Moslems attempt to show that the Christian beliefs in the Trinity, the incarnation, and the atonement are logically absurd and are not proven even in the Bible.

The Trinity is one of the most irrational beliefs for Moslems. Their first argument is that Jesus was not even the Son of God. As noted in the preceding chapter of this book, the Koranic version of his virgin birth differs somewhat from the biblical version. Moslems believe that Mary conceived a child by God's divine will, not through the Holy Spirit.

The second argument concerns Jesus' equality with God the Father. Again, Moslems cite Matthew 19:17 and Mark 10:8 to refute this. "And he [Jesus] said unto him, 'Why callest thou me good? *there is* none good but one, *that is,* God'" (KJV). Furthermore, in John 14:28, Jesus said, "'If ye loved me, ye would rejoice, because I said, I go unto the Father: for my Father is greater than I'" (KJV). Obviously, argue the Moslems, Jesus was not equal to God; in fact, he admitted his own inferiority to God.

The explanation for this misunderstanding on the part of the Moslems was previously discussed. Jesus' dual nature makes him inferior to God the Father as far as his human nature is concerned, but makes him equal to God the Father as far as his divine nature is concerned.

The third argument is that neither Jesus nor the Bible ever mentions the word, "Trinity." Mrs. Ulfat Aziz-Us-Samad, in her book, *A Comparative Study of Christianity and Islam* (1976) cites the 1967 *New Catholic Encyclopedia* to support her view that the doctrine of the Trinity was unknown to early Christians. According to the Encyclopedia, the concept of the Trinity was not solidly established in Christian belief until the end of the fourth century. Furthermore, she argues that Matthew 28:19 is a forgery, as it clearly contradicts other passages. Matthew 28:19 reads, "Go ye therefore, and teach all nations, baptizing them in the name of the Father, and of the Son, and of the Holy Ghost" (KJV). She believes that this verse conflicts with Matthew 10:5, 6, which states, "These twelve Jesus sent forth and commanded them, saying, Go not into the way of the Gentiles, and into *any* city of the Samaritans enter ye not: But go rather to the lost sheep of the house of Israel" (KJV). Mrs. Aziz-Us-Samad goes still further to state that even if Matthew 28:19 was genuine, the mere mention of the Father, the Son, and the Holy Ghost all together does not make them three persons in one Godhead.

Moslems argue, too, that the belief in three persons, each of whom is by himself God, is not compatible with the concept of the oneness of God. Thus, if the Father is God, the Son is God, and the Holy Spirit is God, then God cannot be One, but must be Three. The Christian idea that God is both One and Three at the same time is irrational and illogical. The Koran contains no such irrationality, for it clearly states that there is one unique God who has no partner, and Mohammed is his Prophet.

The basic problem with the Moslem rejection of the Trinity is that such rejection is based on a lack of understanding of the Christian Trinity. Mohammed said, "Say not three; God is one only divinity" (Sura 41:69). No Christian can disagree with this statement, for Christianity is monotheistic in its belief. Moslems must understand that the Trinity does not represent three separate gods. Instead, it represents one God who has revealed his nature to mankind in three separate ways.

The second Christian belief which is completely unacceptable to Moslems is the concept of an incarnate Jesus, i.e., a divine being who assumed the form and nature of a human being. Moslems believe that this is the highest form of blasphemy. They cannot believe that a perfect God would ever need to humble himself by descending into a fleshly form to accomplish his purpose on earth, for God can do all from heaven. Besides that, they argue that if the Father, the Son, and the Holy Spirit are all One, then the Father and the Holy Spirit must have assumed human form when the Son did. Furthermore, if the Son became incarnate at the will of the Father, then the Son was clearly inferior and subordinate to the Father.

Moslems argue, too, that the concept of incarnation places human limitations upon God. Thus, belief in the incarnation of God into a human form denies the infinitude and perfection of God.

Moslems often attack the concept of incarnation on the grounds that it came into Christianity from paganism. They cite the influence of early Babylonian mythology, early Egyptian mythology, Mithraism (an early religion in Persia), and Buddhism. They also point out that Hinduism, even as it is practiced today, resembles Christianity with regard to incarnations. Under Hinduism, Rama and Krishna are Incarnations of Vishnu, the second Person of the Hindu Trinity.

Moslems have contended that early Christians did not accept the dogma of Jesus' divinity. They point out that quite a disagreement arose among the early Christian sects over the divinity question until A.D. 325, when Emperor Constantine pressured opponents of the divinity dogma into silence with his imperial decrees. The Nazarenes, the Ebionites, the Arians, and the Alogians all denied the divinity of Jesus until the church under Constantine forced these people into silence or acquiescence.

The core of this Moslem argument is based upon a misunderstanding concerning the Trinity and Christ's place as the Son of God. Certainly Moslems would agree that God, or Allah, has the power to do anything. Thus, he could most easily be in more than one place at a time. He could manifest a part of his nature in the form of Christ Jesus, the Son, while retaining his other two manifestations in the form of the Father in heaven and the Holy Spirit. Even in the Koran, Mohammed stated that Jesus was the spirit of Allah.

Furthermore, the idea of an incarnate Christ came not from paganism, but from Jesus' own words. In Matthew 16:15–18, Jesus acknowledged that he is the Son of God.

> He said to them, "But who do you say that I am?" And Simon Peter answered and said, "Thou art the Christ, the Son of the living God."
> And Jesus answered and said to him, "Blessed are you, Simon Barjona, because flesh and blood did not reveal this to you, but My Father who is in heaven.
> "And I also say to you that you are Peter, and upon this rock I will build My church; and the gates of Hades shall not overpower it."

Again, in Mark 14:61, 62, Jesus openly states that he is the Son of God.

> But He kept silent, and made no answer. Again the high priest was questioning Him, and saying to Him, "Are You the Christ, the Son of the Blessed One?"
> And Jesus said, "I am; and you shall see the SON OF MAN SITTING AT THE RIGHT HAND OF POWER, and COMING WITH THE CLOUDS OF HEAVEN."

The early "Christian" sects which did not believe in Jesus' divinity were obviously in great error.

The last Christian doctrine untenable to the Moslems is the doctrine of atonement through Jesus' sacrificial blood. Basically Moslems reject the atonement for two reasons. First, they consider the atonement to be a denial of God's mercy and justice. The idea that God would demand the price of innocent blood to forgive men's sins shows a complete lack of mercy. Furthermore, to purposely punish a man (Jesus) who is not guilty of the sins of others, even if he be willing to die for others, is the height of injustice. Besides this, Moslems use Mark 14:36 to show that Jesus really was not completely willing to die for others. In this passage, Jesus said, "'Abba (Father), all things are possible for Thee; remove this cup from me; yet, not what I will, but what Thou wilt.'"

The second reason for the Moslem rejection of the atonement is their contention that Jesus himself never indicated that his death was necessary for salvation. For example, in Matthew 5:44, 45 (KJV), Jesus said:

Love your enemies, bless them that curse you, do good to them that hate you, and pray for them which despitefully use you, and persecute you; that ye may be the children of your Father which is in heaven.

In another Bible passage, Jesus said, "Blessed are the peacemakers; for they shall be called the children of God." Moslems argue that Jesus obviously meant that those who believed in God and performed good works would be saved. They further support this by citing two more Bible passages, Mark 11:25 and Matthew 7:21. In Matthew 6:14, Jesus stated, "If ye forgive men their trespasses, your heavenly Father will also forgive you" (KJV). In Matthew 7:21, Jesus said, "Not everyone who says to Me, 'Lord, Lord,' will enter the kingdom of heaven; but he who does the will of My Father, who is in heaven."

The Moslem arguments here ignore the fact that God is not only full of mercy and justice, but also that he is love. In sending Jesus Christ to earth, God actually sent one manifestation of himself. He was not showing a lack of mercy but rather the highest example of mercy and love. He did not send Jesus to be punished for the sins of others, but rather to bear the burden of others' sins that through one sacrifice, all could be reconciled to him. He also sent Jesus Christ to be a teacher and example for those desiring to serve God.

Jesus' plea and prayer to his Father in the Garden of Gethsemane came from both the human and divine natures. The human side did not want to suffer and die. However, the stronger, divine nature wanted to serve the will of the Father in heaven.

The Royal Mosque (Masdjédé Shah). This mosque, built during the reign of Shah Abbas the Great, is richly decorated both inside and outside with multi-colored mosaics. It is the largest mosque in Isfahan, Iran.

The passages cited by Moslems are taken out of the full context of the Bible. For example, Matthew 7:21 refers to "doing the will of My Father" as the prerequisite for entering God's kingdom. Yet, the will of the Father encompasses all the good works mentioned in other passages. God particularly willed that all believe that Jesus Christ, his Son, was sent to die for the sins of the world, that all men might be saved by believing in him. Furthermore, Jesus himself stated in John 14:6, "'I am the way, and the truth, and the life; no one comes to the Father, but through Me.'"

The Moslem criticisms of Christianity must not be taken lightly. Christians must be intellectually prepared to meet the new challenge of Islam forcefully pushing its way into the Western nations.

A mosque overlooking one of the main squares in Isfahan, Iran

The dome and minarets of Tchahâr Bagh School (Madressé-yé Tchahâr Bagh), theological school built during the reign of Shah Soltan Hossein, the last king of the Safavid dynasty

The Royal Mosque (Masdjédé Shah) built during the reign of Shah
Abbas the Great—the largest mosque in Isfahan, Iran

A courtyard view of the dome and minarets of Tchahâr Bagh School

Entrance to a religious school, the last important architectural work
under Shah Soltan Hossein of the Safavid Dynasty

A cross section of the turquoise mosaic dome of the Tehahâr Bagh
School

Hand-carved work typically found around the entrance doors of
mosques in Iran

View of one minaret at the Tchahâr Bagh School

A view of the Royal Mosque from the terrace of Ali Ghapou in Isfahan, Iran

The Shah's Mosque overlooking the bazaar and craftsman's museum in Isfahan, Iran

8

The Greatest Debate

The sample debate given in this chapter contains a mixture of the contents of numerous debates I have been engaged in with Moslems. Its purpose is to provide both Christians and Moslems with intellectual and spiritual insight into each other's religious beliefs. Imagine now a friendly setting in which two people, one a Moslem and one a Christian, sit together to share and debate ideas on their respective religions.

Christian: Is it not true that the nature of man requires him to search for his Creator? David once said, "As the deer pants for the water brooks, so my soul pants for Thee, O God" (Psalm 42:1).

Moslem: Yes, that is so, but I say as did the great prophet, Mohammed, "How shall I be able to know Thee that I may acquire peace?" It is impossible to know the true nature of Allah, for who has ever seen him? Our prophets taught that anyone who claims to know the nature of the Mighty One is presumptuous and ignorant.

Christian: This is not so according to the truth of the revealed Holy Scriptures. For example, Moses has said that God created man in his own image, to his own

136

likeness (Genesis 1:26). Furthermore, the Holy Scriptures contain Jesus' statement, "Righteous Father, although the world has not known Thee, yet I have known Thee" (John 17:25). He then also stated, "He who has seen Me has seen the Father" (John 14:9).

Moslem: As it is written in our holy book, the Koran, God was neither born nor does he give birth. Why do you Christians make up a story with three gods—God the Father, God the Son, and God the Holy Spirit? This is surely blasphemy not only to us Moslems, but also to the Jews. It is regrettable that your God is different from ours and that all Christians are astray. As it is written, "Do not transgress the bounds of your religion. Speak nothing but the truth about Allah. The Messiah, son of Mary, was no more than Allah's apostle" (Sura 4:171).

Christian: Please allow me to complete your statement from the Koran concerning the Messiah, son of Mary. The full scripture states, "The Messiah, Jesus the son of Mary, was no more than Allah's apostle and His Word which He cast to Mary: a spirit from Him" (Sura 4:171). Thus, you can see that Jesus, the Messiah, was not only the messenger or apostle of God, but he was also the Word and the Spirit of God.

Moslem: Yet Mohammed, the last and greatest prophet of Allah, was the true word of Allah, for through him Allah revealed the true, pure scriptures.

Christian: If this be so, then why did Mohammed himself never claim to be the Word of God? As we search the Koran, we find that he was never more than a messenger of God. It is written, "Mohammed is no more than an apostle; other apostles have died before him" (Sura 3:143).

Moslem: I feel confident from my own Koran that Jesus the Messiah was the messenger of Allah, the word of Allah, and the spirit of Allah. The remaining mystery for

me, however, is why you must call Jesus the Son of God.
What is the meaning of this most mysterious Trinity—
three persons in one? The world of Islam strongly rejects
this illogical notion. It brings nothing but resentment and
enmity between our two religions. Does it not mention in
your Bible that all that you do should be done to the glory
of the Almighty? How then can you justify your pluraliza-
tion of God? Divine reality admits of no division.

Christian: As is well known among the Moslems, one of
the twelve imams was referred to as the "Hand of Allah"
because of his bravery in battles against anti-Moslems.
Moses was known in the Koran as an interlocutor between
man and Allah. Mohammed was called the messenger of
Allah. Furthermore, Jesus was referred to as the Spirit of
Allah. Each bears a title according to his relationship to
and status with Allah. Christians refer to Jesus as the Son
of God because God created him miraculously without any
earthly father. You disagree that God would show himself
in fleshly form on the earth. Yet, Sura 19:14 of the Koran
states with regard to Mary:

> We sent to her Our spirit in the semblance of a full-grown
> man. And when she saw him, she said: "May the Merciful
> defend me from you! If you fear the Lord, leave me and go
> your way."
>
> "I am the messenger of your Lord," he replied, "and have
> come to give you a holy son."
>
> "How shall I bear a child," she answered, "when I am a
> virgin, untouched by man?"
>
> "Such is the will of your Lord," he replied. "That is no
> difficult thing for Him. He shall be a sign to mankind," says
> the Lord, "and a blessing from Ourself. This is our decree."

As you see, then, Allah's spirit did descend in fleshly form
to reveal to Mary that she would have a holy son by Allah's
divine will. This, being true, reveals that Allah's spirit

was both capable and willing to descend at times in the form of a man. Since the Koran calls Jesus the spirit of God, certainly he is God's spirit in fleshly form. He is also, in a unique way, a son conceived by divine will with no earthly father. Is he not then, in this sense, the Son of God? This explains the three manifestations of one God. Why do Moslems reject the predictions of the prophets of the past which stated that Jesus would come as the Son of God?

Moslem: Could you please name a prophet who has already predicted such an event; that is, the coming of Jesus, the Messiah, as the Son of God?

Christian: Yes, of course. Both David and Isaiah prophesied of the coming of the Son of God, of Immanuel, which means God is with us. David said, "The kings of the earth take their stand, And the rulers take counsel together against the Lord and against His Anointed" (Psalm 2:2). He further stated, "Worship the Lord with reverence, And rejoice with trembling. Do homage to the Son, lest He become angry, and you perish in the way, For His wrath may soon be kindled. How blessed are all who take refuge in Him!" (Psalm 2:12). Isaiah prophesied Jesus' birth and true identity as follows: "The Lord Himself will give you a sign: Behold, a virgin will be with child and bear a son, and she will call His name Immanuel" (Isaiah 7:14). The fulfillment of these prophecies has been recorded by the apostles in the Holy Scriptures:

. . . an angel of the Lord appeared to him in a dream, saying, "Joseph, son of David, do not be afraid to take Mary as your wife; for that which has been conceived in her is of the Holy Spirit.

"And she will bear a Son; and you shall call His name Jesus, for it is He who will save His people from their sins."

Now all this took place that what was spoken by the prophet might be fulfilled, saying,

"BEHOLD, THE VIRGIN SHALL BE WITH CHILD, AND SHALL BEAR A SON, AND THEY SHALL CALL HIS NAME IMMANUEL," which translated means,"GOD WITH US" (Matthew 1:20–23).

And Mary said to the angel, "How can this be since I am a virgin?"

And the angel answered and said to her, "The Holy Spirit will come upon you, and the power of the Most High will overshadow you; and for that reason the holy offspring shall be called the Son of God" (Luke 1:34, 35).

God himself spoke from heaven to confirm that Jesus was his Son:

And after being baptized, Jesus went up immediately from the water; and behold, the heavens were opened, and he saw the Spirit of God descending as a dove, and coming upon Him,

and, behold, a voice out of the heavens, saying, "This is My beloved Son, in whom I am well pleased" (Matthew 3:16, 17).

Finally, Jesus himself confirmed during his trial before the Sanhedrin that he was the Son of God:

. . . Again the high priest was questioning Him, and saying . . . , "Are You the Christ, the Son of the Blessed One?" And Jesus said, "I am; . . ." (Mark 14:61, 62).

And they all said, "Are You the Son of God, then?" And He said to them, "Yes, I am" (Luke 22:70).

Moslem: According to your explanation, then, I understand that the claimed sonship of Jesus the Messiah is tied to a spiritual as opposed to an earthly relationship with Allah. We Moslems do not give Jesus the title of Son of God. Nevertheless, I must give some consideration to your point about Allah's spirit appearing in the form of a full-grown man to Mary as written in the Koran. I wish to know more about this concept of the Christian Trinity. You still have not explained how three can be one.

Christian: According to the Koran, as you know, Allah has some 99 different names, each of which represents one of his distinguished qualities. We understand that these 99 qualities are all united into one God. In the same way, in Christianity we call the Almighty God, God the Father, God the Son, and God the Holy Spirit to distinguish between the different manifestations of God. In fact, these manifestations are united into one Being, and we believe in only this one God. Our Scriptures make this clear: "Hear, O Israel! The Lord is our God. The Lord is One!" (Deuteronomy 6:4).

Moslem: I'm trying to grasp the full implications of this. Please show me, though, how three distinct personalities, not just qualities, can be one.

Christian: Let me try to simplify this. No thing existing in this world can be defined in a completely singular sense. We cannot find pure singularity of form in anything. For example, the single substance called water has many forms. Water may be in the form of ice or steam, and yet, it is still the basic substance, water. Similarly, the sea is water, but shows its varied forms in rising waves and splashing droplets. Many other examples can be given, but this should get across my point. God is one Being, but appears in more than one form. If he created so many forms for all substances, why should he choose to remain in only one form? We as humans have several states of being. The first is the physical self which depends upon the biological body. The second is our individual spiritual reality, that is our soul. The third is our individual intellect which is molded greatly by education, experience, and environment. Can man separate himself from or deny any one of these components that make up his total being? Certainly this is impossible. This is the ultimate logical example to convince the human mind of God's oneness in many manifestations without any external partnerships.

Moslem: This is very interesting, but we find Allah to be pure spirit in complete singleness.

Christian: According to the Holy Scriptures, we, too, believe firmly that God is pure spirit. First, it is written:

> In the beginning, God created the heavens and the earth.
> And the earth was formless and void, and darkness was over the surface of the deep; and the Spirit of God was moving over the surface of the waters (Genesis 1:1, 2).

Furthermore, Jesus said, "God is spirit; and those who worship Him must worship in spirit and truth" (John 4:24). Therefore, it is obvious that God is a pure spirit with omnipotent presence. God's spirit has always worked through Jesus, and the Koran itself reveals that Jesus is the spirit of God. God, Jesus, and the Holy Spirit are One, and the spirit (God) has manifested himself each time in a different form. Please listen as I read to you from the Holy Scriptures a few more verses:

> Now there are varieties of gifts, but the same Spirit.
> And there are varieties of ministries, and the same Lord.
> And there are varieties of effects, but the same God who works all things in all persons.
> But to each one is given the manifestation of the Spirit for the common good (1 Corinthians 12:4–7).

As it has been written, your God and my God are one and the same. This same spirit has manifested himself in the forms of the Father, the Son, and the Holy Spirit.

Moslem: I thank you for your explanation of the mysterious Trinity. I have much to contemplate after this discussion. It is really quite interesting. Yet, I must tell you that as Moslems we do not accept what you call the "Holy Scriptures" as the true scriptures. You should know that we believe the Koran to be the last revealed scripture containing the ultimate truth. Your Old and New Testaments, because they were altered by various men, were cast away by Allah and replaced by the Koran.

Christian: Moslems seem not to be aware that the Koran accepts a great portion of our scriptures. In fact, our Holy Scriptures are mentioned 130 times with great respect in your Koran.

Moslem: This may be so, but I need proof that your Bible was not altered before Mohammed's revelations, for Moslems believe that the true gospel has gone to heaven.

Christian: First, I do not understand your last statement. God sent the Holy Scriptures for the guidance of men on earth. Did he then change his mind and take the gospel back to heaven and away from the eyes of earthly men? This is obviously contradictory. Please allow me to mention a few verses from the Koran to show that our Bible has not been altered. Mohammed said,

> Allah has revealed to you the Book with the truth, confirming the scriptures which preceded it; for He has already revealed the Torah and the Gospel for the guidance of men, and the distinction between right and wrong (Sura 3:1, 2).

The Koran also states:

> After those prophets We sent forth Jesus, the son of Mary, confirming the Torah already revealed, and gave him the Gospel, in which there is guidance and light, corroborating

that which was revealed before it in the Torah, a guide and admonition to the righteous (Sura 5:47, 48).

Dear friend, can you really, after this, doubt our Holy Scriptures? If so, let me explain even further. Our Holy Scriptures also have historical authenticity. Fortunately a number of original Greek uncials going back as far as the fourth and fifth centuries have been found. The three most important ones are the *Codex Sinaiticus*, the *Codex Alexandrinus*, and the *Codex Vaticanus*. The *Codex Sinaiticus* is the most complete, for it contains the entire New Testament and a great portion of the Old Testament. One other very important observation with regard to the authenticity of the biblical scriptures is that regardless of the large number of various versions throughout the world, they all agree completely on essential points. It really is quite amazing to realize that the various versions, e.g., Syriac, Latin, Gothic, Armenian, Arabic, Ethiopic, and Coptic, were each made in different countries at different times, and yet agree so completely with each other! This attests to the great care taken in the preparation and transmission of our Holy Scriptures.

Moslem: If your Scriptures are historically authentic and correct, then why do they fail to even mention the great prophet, Mohammed? We recognize Jesus as a great prophet, and yet your Scriptures do not even prophetically tell of his coming after Jesus. They ignore the existence of the greatest messenger of Allah.

Christian: We as Christians respect all religions and have a high regard for the Koran. After all, it contains many of the same scriptural truths as the Bible. Dear friend, where we depart from the teachings of the Koran is at the point where the Koran calls Mohammed the greatest prophet and places him above Jesus, who, as I've shown, was really the Son of God. All prophets from Moses to

David and even to your Mohammed were born of an earthly mother and an earthly father. As noted earlier, the Bible and Koran both reveal that Mary's conception of Jesus was by God's divine will, not by the normal, human, physical act required for conception. Thus, Jesus was unique from all others. He was the ultimate messenger, for he came as the Son of God. The Bible predicts his return to earth for those who believe in him. Thus, our Bible had no prediction of any other messenger, such as Mohammed, to come.

Moslem: But our prophet, Mohammed, did come and did bring the most up-to-date and perfect recording of the holy scriptures that the world has ever had or ever needed. The Koran is a combination of all true scripture revealed, even that scripture prophesying the future up to the end of time.

Christian: If this is true, then no difference between Moslem scriptures and Christian scriptures should exist, for both claim to follow Abraham's religion. Mohammed wrote, "'My Lord has guided me to a straight path, to an upright religion, to the faith of saintly Abraham, who was no idolater'" (Sura 6:161).

Moslem: Well, then, what do your scriptures say about Abraham?

Christian: The full story is recorded in the first book of our Old Testament, Genesis.

> Now when Abram was ninety-nine years old, the Lord appeared to Abram and said to him,
> "I am God the Almighty;
> Walk before Me, and be blameless.
> "And I will establish My covenant between Me and you,
> And I will multiply you exceedingly."
> And Abram fell on his face, and God talked with him, saying,
> "As for Me, behold, My covenant is with you,

And you shall be the father of a multitude of nations.
"No longer shall your name be called Abram,
But your name shall be Abraham;
For I will make you the father of a multitude of nations"
(Genesis 17:1–5).

Moslem: Yes, we, too, believe that Allah blessed
Abraham. We then know that this blessing was later
passed on to Abraham's son, Ishmael.

Christian: I am curious as to why you believe that the
covenant was passed to Ishmael. The Torah explains quite
clearly that God's covenant with Abraham was passed on
to his son, Isaac.

And Abraham said to God, "Oh that Ishmael might live
before Thee!"
But God said, "No, but Sarah your wife shall bear you a
son, and you shall call his name Isaac; and I will establish
My covenant with him for an everlasting covenant for his
descendants after him (Genesis 17:18, 19).

Moslem: Well, actually the Koran does not specifically
state the name of the son who received the covenant, but
the wording indicates that it was Ishmael. The story is
contained in Sura 37:99–112:

We gave him news of a gentle son. And when he reached
the age when he could work with him his father said to him:
"My son, I dreamt that I was sacrificing you. Tell me what
you think."
He replied, "Father, do as you are bidden. Allah willing,
you shall find me faithful."
And when they had both surrendered themselves to
Allah's will, and Abraham had laid down his son prostrate
upon his face, We called out to him, saying, "Abraham, you
have fulfilled your vision." Thus did We reward the righteous. That was indeed a bitter test. We ransomed his son

with a noble sacrifice and bestowed on him the praise of later generations. "Peace be on Abraham!"

Thus are the righteous rewarded. He was one of Our believing servants.

We gave him Isaac, whom We made a saintly prophet, and blessed them both.

We firmly believe that Ishmael, the first born, was the one who withstood the test of Allah and received his covenant after Abraham.

Christian: I would like to refer you to Sura 29:26, which states:

We gave him Isaac and Jacob and bestowed on his descendants prophethood and the Scriptures. We gave him his reward in this life, and in the life to come he shall dwell among the righteous.

This passage out of the Koran seems to confirm that Isaac was the one who received the blessing and Scriptures.

Moslem: Let us not argue this point, for the Koran really is not perfectly clear on it. Regardless of who received God's covenant after Abraham, surely both of Abraham's sons, Ishmael and Isaac, were greatly blessed. What difference does this really make?

Christian: It matters greatly because Jesus' earthly descendants came from Isaac's descendants, and thus, Jesus came from those with whom God had made his original covenant.

Moslem: Well, let us speak now of the greatness of Mohammed as compared to Jesus. Your Holy Scriptures record that Jesus fed a great multitude with two fish and five loaves of bread. Mohammed fed such a multitude once with one small lamb and on another occasion with a handful of dates. Jesus the Messiah commanded Peter by the power of faith to walk upon the water. Yet, Mohammed commanded a great stone to roll across the waters to him. Besides this, Mohammed's miracles exceeded even those of Moses. The Scriptures record that Moses once obtained water enough for his people by striking a rock. Yet, Mohammed let a small trickle of water flow from his blessed fingers so much that 5,500 thirsty men could drink during the Battle Ahad. Mohammed performed many other such miracles which were the greatest of all times.

Christian: I have studied the religion of Islam for years and I'm afraid to say that I've never seen any such miracles by Mohammed recorded in your scriptures. Can you please show me where this is found in the Koran?

Moslem: Although these miracles are not listed in the Koran, they are well known through recorded Islamic tradition.

Christian: Well, you yourself previously stated that you did not want to rely upon recorded tradition alone. Just as you prefer to stick to the Koran, so do I on this matter. Please remember Sura 29:49 where Mohammed gives an answer to the question of why he was given no signs by Allah.

> They ask: "Why has no sign been given him by his Lord?" Say: "Signs are in the hands of Allah. My mission is only to give plain warning."
>
> Is it not enough for them that We have revealed to you the Book for their instruction? Surely in this there is a blessing and an admonition to true believers.

Furthermore, in Sura 5:110–111, the Koran mentions by name some of the many miracles that Jesus performed:

> Allah will say: "Jesus, son of Mary, remember the favour I have bestowed on you and on your mother: how I strengthened you with the Holy Spirit, so that you preached in your cradle and in the prime of manhood; how I instructed you in the Scriptures and in wisdom, in the Torah and in the

Gospel; how by My leave you fashioned from clay the likeness of a bird and breathed into it so that, by My leave, it became a living bird; how, by My leave, you healed the blind man and the leper, and by My leave restored the dead to life; how I protected you from the Israelites when you brought them veritable signs: when the unbelievers among them said: "This is nothing but plain magic. . . ."

Please reflect upon all of this for a moment. The Koran attributes no miracles to Mohammed other than the writing of the Book, but it lists numerous miracles performed by Jesus.

Moslem: All right. I will accept what you have brought from the Koran here. However, I must now ask you that if you bring so much evidence from our own Holy Book, how can you say that Jesus was crucified on a cross? Our holy scriptures reveal that Jesus was neither killed nor crucified, but someone similar in appearance was seized and crucified. Would Allah allow such a wonderful and great prophet to suffer in such a terrible way? No! In fact, later Allah simply raised Jesus up into heaven. Please hear the words of the Koran here:

They denied the truth and uttered a monstrous falsehood against Mary. They declared: "We have put to death the Messiah Jesus the son of Mary, the apostle of Allah." They did not kill him, nor did they crucify him, but they thought they did.

Those that disagreed about him were in doubt concerning his death, for what they knew about it was sheer conjecture; they were not sure that they had slain him. Allah lifted him up to His presence; He is mighty and wise (Sura 41:156–158).

Christian: Your Koran mentions that there was sheer conjecture regarding whether or not Jesus actually was crucified. Yet, the Holy Scriptures contain numerous eyewitness accounts written by Jesus' own apostles and

closest friends that confirm the fact that he was crucified
on a cross. Searching our Holy Scriptures, we find as
noted earlier that many prophets predicted the coming of
Jesus, the Son of God. Others predicted his crucifixion to
save men from their sins.

> He was despised and forsaken of men,
> A man of sorrows, and acquainted with grief;
> And like one from whom men hide their face,
> He was despised, and we did not esteem Him.
> Surely our griefs He Himself bore,
> And our sorrows He carried;
> Yet we ourselves esteemed Him stricken,
> Smitten of God, and afflicted.
> But He was pierced through for our transgressions,
> He was crushed for our iniquities;
> The chastening of our well-being fell upon Him,
> And by His scourging we are healed (Isaiah 53:3–6).

> For dogs have surrounded me;
> A band of evildoers has encompassed me;
> They pierced my hands and my feet.
> I can count all my bones.
> They look, they stare at me;
> They divide my garments among them,
> And for my clothing they cast lots (Psalm 22:16–18).

If you do not wish to accept our Scriptures, then you
must at least consider the historical evidence, that is,
evidence found in the writings of objective historians of
the era in which Jesus lived. For example, the *Annals* of
Tacitus, the *Biographies* of Seutonius, and the *Letters* of
Pliny all attest to the factual death of Jesus Christ under
Pontius Pilate and the rapid growth of those who worshiped Christ as God. It is unfortunate that Moslems have
been so intent on denying Christian belief concerning
Jesus Christ that they have overlooked much written,

historical evidence of Jesus' crucifixion and subsequent resurrection.

Moslem: I have noted your point of view on this matter. Now I wish for you to note a matter of grave importance to us Moslems. We believe that Jesus predicted the coming of another prophet after him for the guidance of mankind. This is recorded in both the Koran and the Bible.

> And of Jesus, who said to the Israelites: "I am sent forth to you by Allah to confirm the Torah already revealed and to give news of an apostle that will come after me whose name is Ahmed" (Sura 61:6).

> "And I will ask the Father, and He will give you another Helper, that He may be with you forever; . . ." (John 14:16).

Christian: I am pleased that you now bring up this subject with reference to our Holy Scriptures.

Moslem: Please let me continue with one further verse to complete my point. John 16:7 states:

> But I tell you the truth, it is to your advantage that I go away; for if I do not go away, the Helper shall not come to you; but if I go, I will send Him to you.

Christian: Dear friend, I see the basic conflict here. I have studied the Bible thoroughly, but have never seen the name, Ahmed (Mohammed) mentioned in it. You quoted John 14:16, but did not go on to finish the thought with John 14:17, which states:

> that is the spirit of truth, whom the world cannot receive, because it does not behold Him or know Him, but you know Him because He abides with you, and will be in you.

This clearly shows that the Helper referred to in verse 16 could not have been an earthly being such as Mohammed.

The Helper was definitely a spirit, that is, the Holy Spirit which could not be seen by men, but which would dwell within men. The Scripture also makes it clear that the Helper, or Holy Spirit, would neither leave men nor die. It indwells each soul eternally. Obviously this was not the case with Mohammed. In Luke 24:49 Jesus instructed his disciples to remain in Jerusalem a short period of time after his death until the Holy Spirit would descend upon them. Acts 2:1–4 records the actual appearance of the Holy Spirit when it came upon the disciples:

> And when the day of Pentecost had come, they were all together in one place.
> And suddenly there came from heaven a noise like a violent, rushing wind, and it filled the whole house where they were sitting.
> And there appeared to them tongues as of fire distributing themselves, and they rested on each one of them.
> And they were filled with the Holy Spirit and began to speak with other tongues, as the Spirit was giving them utterance.

Moslem: Thank you for your explanation regarding your concept of the Helper. Can you really prove, though, that Jesus was the only and the ultimate savior for all mankind?

Christian: First, this was revealed in the Torah as follows:

> Thus says the Lord, the King of Israel
> And his Redeemer, the Lord of hosts:
> "I am the first and I am the last,
> And there is no God besides Me" (Isaiah 44:6).

Peter, Jesus' apostle, stated:

> "The God of our fathers raised up Jesus, whom you had put to death by hanging Him on a cross.

He is the one whom God exalted to His right hand as a Prince and a Savior, to grant repentance to Israel, and forgiveness of sins" (Acts 5:30, 31).

Other scriptures reveal what Jesus himself said on this subject:

Jesus said to him, "I am the way, and the truth, and the life; no one comes to the Father but through Me" (John 14:6).

And Jesus came up and spoke to them, saying, "All authority has been given to Me in heaven and on earth.
"Go therefore and make disciples of all the nations, baptizing them in the name of the Father and the Son, and the Holy Spirit,
teaching them to observe all that I commanded you; and lo, I am with you always, even to the end of the age" (Matthew 28:18–20).

Then if any one says to you, "Behold, here is the Christ," or "There He is," do not believe him.
For false Christs and false prophets will arise and show great signs and wonders, so as to mislead, if possible, even the elect (Matthew 24:23, 24).

Moslem: You say that Jesus is the Savior, the first and the last. However, our scriptures are directly in conflict with this. The Koran specifically states that Mohammed came as the last and greatest prophet.

Christian: How could anyone be greater than Jesus who came as the Spirit of God in love to innocently give his life for the remission of all men's sins? As stated in 2 Corinthians 5:21, Jesus was without sin. He was pure and innocent. He came as an example of godliness.

Therefore, be imitators of God, as beloved children;
and walk in love, just as Christ also loved you, and gave

Himself up for us, an offering and a sacrifice to God as a fragrant aroma (Ephesians 5:1, 2).

Moslem: Certainly I believe that Jesus was innocent and pure, but so were all of the prophets of Allah. They all walked among the people and eloquently revealed to the people what Allah had revealed to them. Each, in his mission to spread Allah's revelations, was just and without sin.

Christian: If we study the scriptural life stories of the prophets, such as Abraham, Moses, Solomon, and David, we will find that none claimed to be without sin. In fact, quite the contrary was true. On several occasions, each sought the forgiveness of God. For example, in Psalm 25:11, David stated: "For Thy name's sake, O Lord, pardon my iniquity, for it is great."

Moslem: Here our beliefs differ. We Moslems believe that the prophets, especially Mohammed, were the highest men on earth and that they intercede for men before Allah. We bury our dead near the burial sites of past prophets whenever possible so that they will be near an intercessor. Even after death, the prophets act as intecessors between men and Allah. Do Christians not believe that the prophets are intercessors for men?

Christian: No, we do not. I do not really understand how you believe this either, especially if you read Sura 2:47 of your own Koran. It states:

> Children of Israel, remember the blessing I have bestowed on you, and that I have exalted you above the nations. Guard yourselves against the day when every soul shall stand alone: when neither intercession nor ransom shall be accepted from it, nor any help be given to it.

Furthermore, Mohammed himself said that he was no prodigy among the apostles.

I am no prodigy among the apostles; nor do I know what will be done with me or you. I follow only what is revealed to me, and my only duty is to give plain warning (Sura 46:10).

Moslem: If Christians do not believe that the prophets are intercessors, then must all stand alone before Allah on the Day of Judgment?

Christian: Our Holy Scriptures reveal that indeed we shall have one true intercessor all through our lives, even on the Day of Judgment.

My little children, I am writing these things to you that you may not sin. And if anyone sins, we have an Advocate with the Father, Jesus Christ the righteous;

and He Himself is the propitiation for our sins; and not for ours only, but also for those of the whole world (1 John 2:1, 2).

Jesus himself, in speaking to God the Father, stated:

Father, I desire that they also, whom Thou hast given Me, be with Me where I am, in order that they may behold My glory, which Thou hast given Me; for Thou didst love Me before the foundation of the world (John 17:24).

Jesus also promised all who follow him, ". . . lo, I am with you always, even to the end of the age" (Matthew 28:20). Does your Koran reflect such purity of love as this? It strikes me as being a book which concentrates on punishment, fright, and doom. Our scriptures encourage all to share God's love through Jesus Christ so that we willingly, with great love, obey God. We serve out of love, not fear.

For you have not received a spirit of slavery leading to fear again, but have received a spirit of adoption as sons by which we cry out, "Abba! Father!" (Romans 8:15).

By this, love is perfected with us, that we may have confidence in the day of judgment; because as He is, so also are we in this world.

There is no fear in love; but perfect love casts out fear, because fear involves punishment, and the one who fears is not perfected in love (1 John 4:17, 18).

Let us see now what Mohammed has said in the Koran, which reveals the Moslem philosophy and compare it to what Jesus has said. Sura 9:4, 5 states:

Proclaim a woeful punishment to the unbelievers, except those idolaters who have honoured their treaties with you and aided none against you. With these keep faith until their treaties have run their term. Allah loves the righteous.

When the sacred months are over slay the idolaters wherever you find them. Arrest them, besiege them, and lie in ambush everywhere for them.

Other such teachings are as follows:

Prophet, make war on the unbelievers and the hypocrites and deal rigorously with them (Sura 9:73).

Believers, take neither Jews nor Christians for your friends. They are friends with one another. Whoever of you seeks their friendship shall become one of their number (Sura 5:51).

In contrast, Jesus has said:

You have heard that it was said, "You shall love your neighbor, and hate your enemy."

But I say to you, love your enemies, and pray for those who persecute you (Matthew 5:43, 44).

But I say to you who hear, love your enemies, do good to those who hate you, bless those who curse you, pray for those who mistreat you (Luke 6:27, 28).

Christians have been instructed to pray for unbelievers and gently but perseveringly guide them to the truth. Any judgment or punishment of unbelievers comes from God alone. Jesus the Savior was the ultimate example of Christian love, for even as he gave his life for the sinners of the world, he looked down from the cross at those who taunted him and cast lots for his clothing, and he stated simply:

Father, forgive them; for they do not know what they are doing (Luke 23:34).

Moslem: I thank you for sharing your philosophy and beliefs with me today. I hope our discussion gave you some insights into our beliefs also. I have much to contemplate after this, for I have never really heard Christianity explained in this way before.

Christian: I pray and trust that God will guide you as well as me in our future contemplations.

9

The Growing Challenge to Christianity

The Moslems—Where Are They?

Iran, which has been discussed in this book, is approximately 90 percent Moslem, 5 percent Christian, 3 percent Jewish, and 2 percent Zoroastrian and Bahai.

Tips to Christians on Converting Moslems

Having been directed by God to teach unbelievers, all Christians are missionaries. God did not make this an option to Christians, but gave it to them as a direct command.

Christians, both at home and abroad, are needed to meet the growing challenge of Islam. The following is a list of the most important things Christians need to do *before* beginning their mission to convert Moslems:

(1) Read and thoroughly study the Koran. Those planning to go to a Moslem country should learn to say in Arabic the most important Koranic passages, that is, those passages differing substantially from the Bible. Moslems are often offended by translations of the Koran from the original Arabic. If not offended, at least they probably will not trust the accuracy of a translated version.

Where the Moslems Are:	
United States 2,000,000	
USSR...40,000,000	
China..17,000,000	

Moslem Population More Than 90 percent:	
Afghanistan	Mauritania
Algeria	Morocco
Egypt	Oman
Gambia	Pakistan
Iran	Saudi Arabia
Iraq	Somalia
Jordan	Tunisia
Libya	Turkey
	Yemen

A majority of the people in 57 nations are Moslems

(2) Show respect for the Moslem Koran and the Prophet Mohammed. The Moslems have great respect for Jesus as a prophet and resent the Christian's complete ignorance of their prophet, Mohammed.

(3) Although many questions thrown at Christians by Moslems are very difficult to answer, the Christian should be prepared through diligent study to answer all questions in a way which Moslems will understand. In other words, the Christian must be familiar with all difficult questions and be ready to handle them in a context showing that he is familiar with how the Moslems view certain Christian concepts.

(4) The prospective foreign missionary must not only learn the language of the Moslem country he plans to enter, but he must also learn as much as possible about the body language that accompanies speech. Part of this includes such things as the speaking distance between two people. Many times, native English speakers or Western Europeans have been backed into a wall by native Arab speakers simply because the normal speaking distance for Arabs is much closer than that for native English speakers and Western Europeans. Not knowing such things as this can easily cause distraction and even hostility on the part of one or both parties. At the very least, it hinders communication.

(5) The prospective foreign missionary must also familiarize himself with the new country's culture. For example, in most Moslem countries, greetings and handshaking are extremely important. If one should meet even a casual acquaintance three or four times in one day, each takes the time to give a friendly greeting and unhurried handshake. The ignorance of this custom, for whatever reason, is a great offense to Moslems.

Obviously all matters pertaining to language, body language, and culture cannot be included here. Each prospective missionary is responsible for researching and learning these things. Those remaining at home who are interested in converting Moslems must at least study the English version of the Koran in depth as well as the Bible and compare the two. They also must prepare themselves to meet the often difficult questions asked by Moslems. Most public and university libraries presently have books on both Islam and Christianity. Many also have comparative books on the two religions. Such study can prepare the Christian not only to answer Moslems' questions, but also to challenge Moslems with questions from Christians.

One last word on this subject is necessary. Too many

Christian missionaries, both domestic and foreign, have failed to properly equip themselves *ahead of time* for their work. Eagerness to spread God's Word is not enough. The old saying that all one needs is faith in God and knowledge of the Bible to spread the Word may be true for teaching in one's own culture, but it has been proven wrong when applied to Moslem countries. The statistics show the great failure rate of past Christian missionaries in such countries. The primary problem is lack of adequate preparation before entrance into the Moslem country. Once the missionary reaches the country, he begins to learn the language and customs, but alienates many Moslems through his mistakes during his first four or five years there. If the prospective missionary wishes to study the language and culture in the country where he will be working, then he should do so as a *student,* not as a full-fledged missionary. Once he has learned the language, customs, and the Koran and has gathered a circle of friends, then he is in a proper position to begin his formal missionary work.

A Plea to the Church

Brothers and sisters in Christ, we must unite and become like the church of Macedonia. Paul said of this church, "For I testify that according to their ability, and beyond their ability they gave of their own accord, begging us with much entreaty for the favor of participation in the support of the saints" (2 Corinthians 8:3, 4). The early Macedonian Christians not only gave beyond their ability, but they also gave because they *desired* to give to the Lord's work. A very important word here is "desire." Only too often in this era, Christians confuse sincere desire to serve God with either a guilt feeling that one must serve God or with fear that others may think he is ungiving in the community of Christ. Remember Paul's words, "Let each one do just as he has purposed in his heart; not grudgingly or under compulsion; for God loves a cheerful giver."

Brethren, the time for us to honestly evaluate our God-given role on earth is past due. Each individual must ask himself, "Can God use me better in local mission or in foreign mission work?" If the answer appears to be that he cannot use me in any mission work, or that I am too busy for any mission work, then something is definitely wrong. We must remember that our purpose for being here is to glorify God and bring others to his truth. The earthly jobs that materially sustain our lives are important, but they cannot even begin to compete with God's job for us.

Brethren, if you cannot enter a foreign mission field because you honestly feel that God has not prepared you or called you for such work, then please at least think of how you, here at home, can feed the Word to those abroad. Paul stated in 2 Corinthians 9:10, "Now He who supplies seed to the sower and bread for food, will supply and multiply your seed for sowing and increase the harvest of your righteousness."

Remember, brethren, that the main goal of every Christian is not to make the world materially a better and more comfortable place in which to live, but rather to carry on the Lord's mission—to teach and preach the gospel to every nation. Under the present conditions of the world, the children of God should reflect on a permanent world-wide victory in order to meet the challenge of the age. All Christians must join together to start a world revolution which is not based on arms and hate but rather on love, peace, and the salvation of all human souls.

Bibliography

Al-Qaderi, F. R. A., Ph.D. *Islam and Christianity in the Modern World*. 2nd ed. Karachi, Pakistan: Trade Industry Publications, LTD, 1976.

Aziz-Us-Samad, Mrs. Ulfat. *A Comparative Study of Christianity and Islam*. 3rd ed. Lahore, Pakistan: S. H. Muhammed Asraf, 1976.

Chishti, Yousuf Saleem. *What Is Christianity*. Karachi, Pakistan: World Federation of Islamic Missions, 1970.

Delury, George E., ed. *The World Almanac and Book of Facts 1979*. New York: Newspaper Enterprise Association, Inc., 1978.

Hefley, James and Marti. *Arabs, Christians, Jews*. Plainfield, N.J.: Logos International, 1978.

"The Muslims Are Coming . . . Is That A Mosque in Your Neighborhood?" *Eternity*, 1978.

The Koran. Translated by N. J. Dawood. New York: Penguin Books, 1956.

New American Standard Bible. La Habra, Calif.: Foundation Press Publications, 1960.

Robinson, Maxine. *Mohammed*. New York: Vintage Books, 1974.

Schumaker, Richard, "Oil Money Now Spreads Islam." *Eternity*, Sept. 1979.

Smith, Wilbur M., D.D. *The Supernaturalness of Christ*. Boston: Wilde Co., 1954.

Wood, Barry. *Questions Non-Christians Ask*. Old Tappan, N.J.: Fleming H. Revell Co., 1960.

The World Book Encyclopedia. Chicago: Field Enterprises Educational Corp., 1976.